EYEWITNESS
UNIVERSE

Hubble Space Telescope

High-energy particle tracks

Magellan Venus orbiter

Jupiter and its moon Io

Martian volcano

The surface of Mars

Bust of
Jupiter

Chandra X-ray
satellite

EYEWITNESS
UNIVERSE

Written by
ROBIN KERROD

A galaxy about 23 million light-years away

Core of an
active galaxy

Mars

Spectroscope

DK | Penguin
Random
House

Project editor Giles Sparrow
Art editor Tim Brown
Senior editor Kitty Blount
Senior art editor Martin Wilson
Managing editor Andrew Macintyre
Managing art editor Jane Thomas
Category Publisher Linda Martin
Art director Simon Webb
Production Erica Rosen
Picture research Sean Hunter
DTP Designer Siu Yin Ho

RELAUNCH EDITION (DK UK)
Editor Ashwin Khurana
US editor Margaret Parrish
Managing editor Gareth Jones
Managing art editor Philip Letsu
Publisher Andrew Macintyre
Producer, pre-production Adam Stoneham
Senior producer Janis Griffith
Jacket editor Maud Whatley
Jacket designer Laura Brim
Jacket development manager Sophia MTT
Publishing director Jonathan Metcalf
Associate publishing director Liz Wheeler
Art director Phil Ormerod

RELAUNCH EDITION (DK INDIA)
Editor Ishani Nandi
Project art editor Deep Shikha Walia
Art editor Amit Varma
Senior DTP designer Harish Aggarwal
DTP designer Pawan Kumar
Managing editor Alka Thakur Hazarika
Managing art editor Romi Chakraborty
CTS manager Balwant Singh
Jacket designers Suhita Dharamjit, Sukriti Sobti
Managing jacket editor Saloni Singh

Earth

First American Edition, 2003
This American Edition, 2015
Published in the United States by DK Publishing
345 Hudson Street, New York, New York 10014

Copyright © 2003, © 2009, © 2015
Dorling Kindersley Limited
A Penguin Random House Company
15 16 17 18 19 10 9 8 7 6 5 4 3 2 1
001—280089—Mar/2015

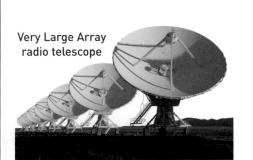

Very Large Array
radio telescope

Sunrise at Stonehenge

A catalog record for this book is available
from the Library of Congress.

ISBN: 978-1-4654-3187-5 (PB)
ISBN: 978-1-4654-3362-6 (ALB)

DK books are available at special discounts when purchased
in bulk for sales promotions, premiums, fund-raising, or
educational use. For details, contact: DK Publishing Special
Markets, 345 Hudson Street, New York, New York 10014
SpecialSales@dk.com

Color reproduction by Alta Image Ltd., London, UK
Printed and bound by South China Printing Co. Ltd., China

All images © Dorling Kindersley Limited

For further information see: www.dkimages.com

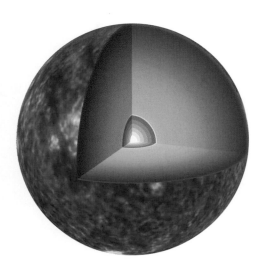

Inside a supergiant star

Interior of Jupiter

A WORLD OF IDEAS:
SEE ALL THERE IS TO KNOW

Contents

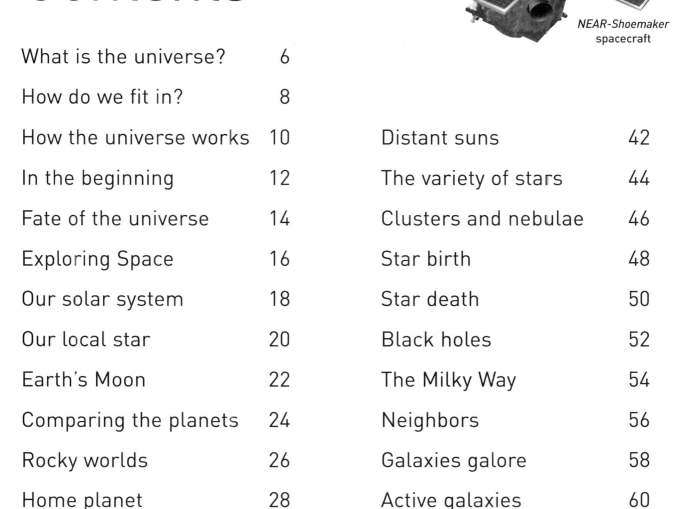

NEAR-Shoemaker spacecraft

What is the universe?

The universe is everything that exists—today, in the past, and in the future. It is an immense space populated by innumerable galaxies of stars and permeated with light and other radiation. When we look at the night sky, we are peering into the fathomless depths of the universe and stars that are trillions of miles away. Humans have been studying the universe for at least 5,000 years, through the science of astronomy.

Spaceship Earth
The *Apollo 8* astronauts were the first people to see our planet floating alone in the universe, as they headed for the Moon in 1968. The Earth is important to us Earthlings, but insignificant in the universe as a whole.

"The history of astronomy is a history of receding horizons."

EDWIN HUBBLE
DISCOVERER OF GALAXIES
BEYOND OUR OWN

Early astronomy
The ancient Britons knew about the movements of the Sun, Moon, and stars. In around 2600 BCE, they completed Stonehenge: circles of standing stones that marked the positions of the Sun and Moon during the year.

Babylonian astrological tablet

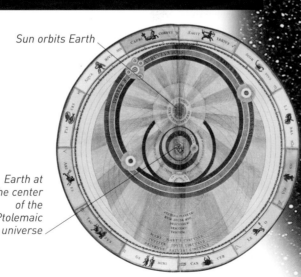

Sun orbits Earth

Earth at the center of the Ptolemaic universe

Astrology
Ancient Babylonians thought that things that happened in space could affect humans on Earth. This line of belief is called astrology and is still followed today.

Ptolemy's universe
In around 150 CE, the Alexandrian-Greek astronomer Ptolemy wrongly theorized that the Earth was at the center of the universe and everything else moved around it.

World in motion

In 1543, Nicolaus Copernicus theorized a Sun-centered universe where the Earth and the other planets travel around the Sun in circular orbits. Later, German Johannes Kepler discovered that the planets travel around the Sun not in circles, but in ellipses.

Johannes Kepler
(1571–1630)

Neptune Saturn   Earth   Sun   Mars   Jupiter   Uranus

Hand-wound
mechanism

Mechanical
model (orrery) of
the solar system

Planetary pathway

Kepler's laws of planetary motion explained that the planets move around the Sun. In 1687, Isaac Newton found that it was a force called gravity that kept the planets in the Sun's orbit.

Stars and galaxies

By the late 1700s, astronomers began to work out what our galaxy was like. By plotting the distribution of stars, William Herschel proved that our galaxy is lens-shaped (it is, in fact, a bulging spiral). In 1923, Edwin Hubble discovered the first galaxy outside our own: the Andromeda "nebula."

*Andromeda
is a spiral
galaxy*

*Stars in
our galaxy*

The Andromeda
Galaxy, M31

Everything's relative

Early in the last century, German physicist Albert Einstein transformed our ideas about space and the universe. He presented two theories of relativity—the special theory in 1905 and the general theory 10 years later. The theories show that nothing can move faster than the speed of light, and that energy and mass are equivalent and can be converted into each other.

A field of galaxies whose
light has taken up to
10 billion years to reach us

How do we fit in?

Not long ago, people thought our planet was the center of the universe. In fact, it is an insignificant rock in a small galaxy, in one tiny corner of space. No one knows how big the universe is, but objects have been detected 76 sextillion miles (123 million million billion km) away—a distance beyond our comprehension.

Medieval world map

Pancake planet
Before the 15th-century era of discovery and exploration, people assumed the Earth was flat—go too far and you would fall over the edge.

Scale of the universe
Our insignificance in the universe is shown in these images, from life at the human scale to the immensity of intergalactic space. We use the light-year—5.9 trillion miles (9.5 trillion km)—to measure distances in space.

From space, Earth looks blue because of the vast expanses of surface water. White clouds surround the planet.

The Oort Cloud of cometlike bodies forms a boundary around the solar system. At the speed of light, it would take more than a year and a half to reach the outer edge of the Oort Cloud.

Runners in a marathon cross a crowded bridge.

A satellite in orbit, hundreds of miles above Earth, looks down on the city.

Our view of the universe
We look out at the universe from inside a layer of stars that forms the disk of our galaxy. Along the plane of this disk, the galaxy extends for tens of thousands of light-years. In the night sky, we see this dense band as the Milky Way. By combining different satellite images of the sky, we can see what the universe looks like from inside our Galaxy (left).

In the solar system, Earth lies three planets out from the Sun. It would take more than eight minutes to travel to the Sun at the speed of light.

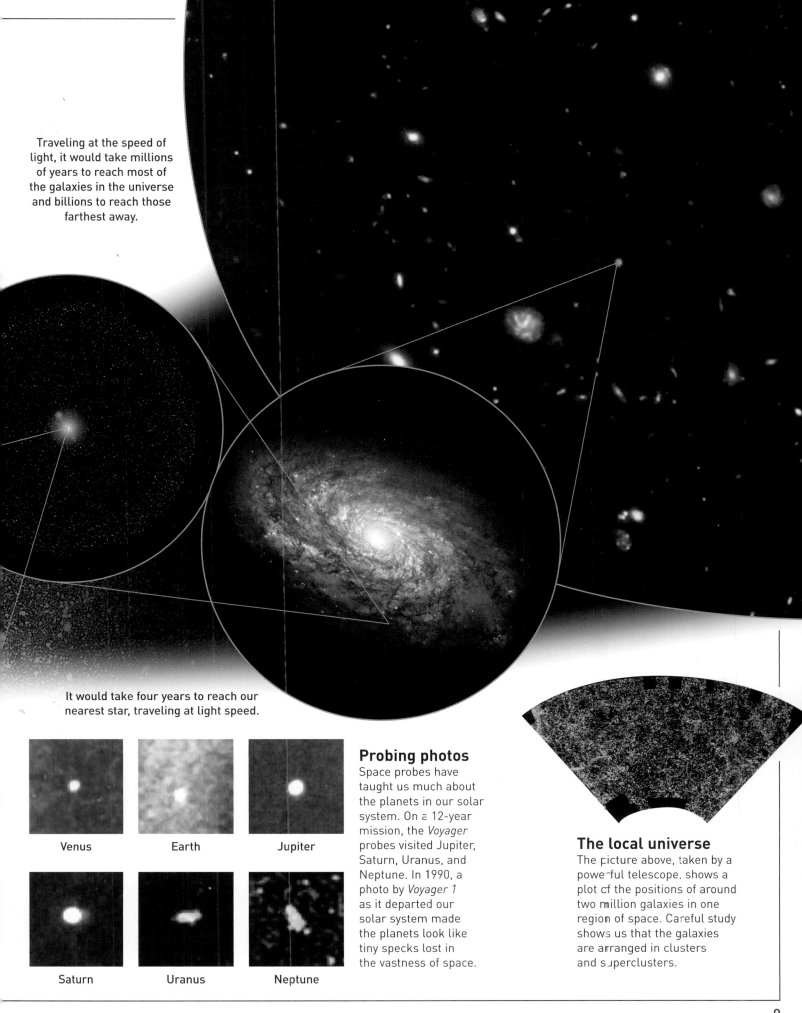

Traveling at the speed of light, it would take millions of years to reach most of the galaxies in the universe and billions to reach those farthest away.

It would take four years to reach our nearest star, traveling at light speed.

Venus

Earth

Jupiter

Saturn

Uranus

Neptune

Probing photos

Space probes have taught us much about the planets in our solar system. On a 12-year mission, the *Voyager* probes visited Jupiter, Saturn, Uranus, and Neptune. In 1990, a photo by *Voyager 1* as it departed our solar system made the planets look like tiny specks lost in the vastness of space.

The local universe

The picture above, taken by a powerful telescope, shows a plot of the positions of around two million galaxies in one region of space. Careful study shows us that the galaxies are arranged in clusters and superclusters.

How the universe works

The universe is made up of islands of matter in an ocean of empty space. Energy travels through the universe as light and other radiation. Four fundamental forces dictate what matter is like and how it behaves. The strongest of the four binds particles together, while the weakest, gravity, holds the universe together.

Water droplet

Water molecule made from one oxygen and two hydrogen atoms

Protons have a positive electric charge

Inside an atom, electrons orbit a tiny nucleus

Neutrons have no charge

Electrons have a negative electric charge

Inside atoms
Atoms are made up of tiny, subatomic particles. The three main particles are protons and neutrons, found inside an atom's nucleus, and electrons, which circle it.

Protons and neutrons are made up of even tinier particles called quarks

Elements and atoms
Empedocles believed matter was made up of fire, air, water, and earth. His fellow Greek philosopher, Democritus, thought instead that matter was made of tiny bits he called atoms. Hundreds of years later, English chemist John Dalton confirmed Democritus's theory.

Empedocles

Radio waves (wavelengths 1 mm or more)

Peak

Trough

Trough

Wavelength

A family of waves
The radiation that carries energy through the universe takes the form of electromagnetic waves. There are many kinds of radiation, differing in wavelength—the distance between one peak or trough of the wave and the next. Visible light is radiation that our eyes see as colors from violet to red, with wavelengths between 390 and 700 nanometers (one nanometer is a billionth of a meter). Invisible wavelengths are shorter than violet light and longer than red.

Particle tracks as seen at a European nuclear research center in Geneva

Similar poles of magnets repel each other

Iron filings reveal invisible lines of magnetic field

Probing the atom
Physicists use incredibly powerful machines called particle accelerators, or "atom smashers," to investigate the structure of atoms. These machines accelerate beams of subatomic particles and smash them into atoms.

Magnetism
Magnetism is the force that makes magnets attract iron filings. When suspended, a magnet will align itself north-south, in the direction of our planet's magnetic field. Earth's magnetism extends far out into space, creating a bubblelike region called the magnetosphere.

Grades of gravity

Scientist Isaac Newton established the basic law of gravity: that every body attracts every other body because of its mass. The bigger a body, the greater its gravitational attraction. Saturn's enormous gravity keeps rings of particles circling its equator and over 62 moons in orbit around it.

Saturn, its rings, and three of its satellites photographed by the Hubble Space Telescope

"The most incomprehensible thing about the world is that it is comprehensible."

ALBERT EINSTEIN

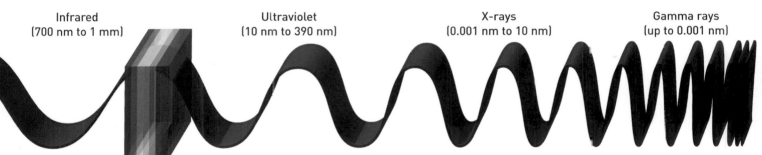

Infrared
(700 nm to 1 mm)

Ultraviolet
(10 nm to 390 nm)

X-rays
(0.001 nm to 10 nm)

Gamma rays
(up to 0.001 nm)

Visible light
(390 nm to 700 nm)

Europe's infrared observatory ISO

ISO view of Rho Ophiuchi star-forming region

The hidden universe

We see the universe as it appears in visible light. But the universe also gives out radiation at invisible wavelengths. Invisible radiations can be studied only from space, using satellites.

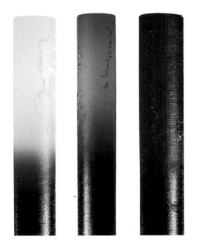

Energy and light

When you heat up an iron poker in a fire, the iron gives out shorter wavelengths (colors) of light. It is the same in space—the coolest red stars have a temperature under 5,500°F (3,000°C), while the hottest blue-white stars have temperatures 10 times greater.

In the beginning

We have a good idea of what the universe is like today and what makes it tick. But where did it come from? How has it evolved? What will happen to it in the future? The branch of astronomy that studies these questions is called cosmology. Cosmologists believe that an explosive event called the Big Bang created the universe around 13.8 billion years ago. They are not so certain about how the universe might end (see p. 14).

What came before?
Unlike a baby that grows into an adult, all the material of the universe was created in one moment during the Big Bang. Nothing existed before the Big Bang.

Big Bang creates the universe, which is infinitely small, infinitely hot, and full of energy

Energy from the Big Bang creates particles of matter and antimatter, which annihilate one another

As the universe cools, combinations of particles become stable

Evolving universe
Three minutes after the Big Bang, the temperature of the universe fell from countless trillion trillions of degrees to a billion degrees. This cooling allowed the conversion of energy into the subatomic particles that would seed the first galaxies 300,000 years later.

A fraction of a second into its life, the universe expands to an enormous size

As the universe cools down, quarks become the dominant type of matter

Quarks collide to form protons and neutrons

Electrons and positron particles form

Matter too dense for light to travel freely

Light waves bounce off particles before traveling far, just as in a fog

Temperature drops and electrons are soaked up into atoms

Most electrons and positrons annihilate each other

Universe expanding from Big Bang

Temperature is steadily dropping

Matter condenses to form galaxies and clusters

Georges Lemaître
Around 1930, Belgian astronomer Georges Lemaître suggested that the universe was created in a single moment when a "primeval atom" exploded. Lemaître's ideas laid the foundation for the Big Bang theory.

Clear universe
Until the universe was about 300,000 years old, it was full of particles and opaque. Then electrons combined with atomic nuclei to form the first atoms. The particles then cleared, and the universe became transparent.

Photons now travel freely in largely empty space

Decoupling photons are the earliest we can detect

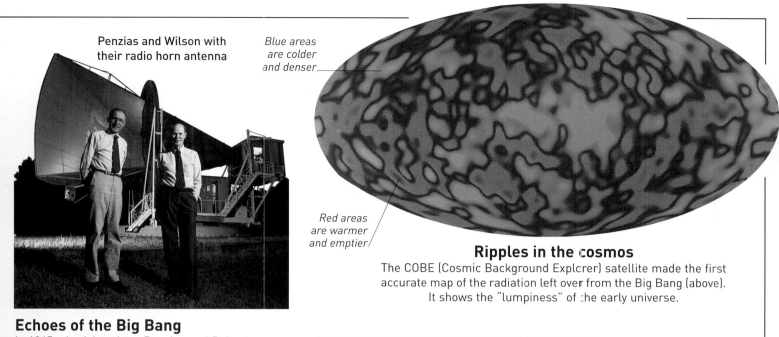

Penzias and Wilson with their radio horn antenna

Blue areas are colder and denser

Red areas are warmer and emptier

Ripples in the cosmos

The COBE (Cosmic Background Explorer) satellite made the first accurate map of the radiation left over from the Big Bang (above). It shows the "lumpiness" of the early universe.

Echoes of the Big Bang

In 1965, physicists Arno Penzias and Robert Wilson picked up weak radio signals coming from the sky with a cosmic background temperature of around -454°F (-270°C). This is the temperature scientists calculated would follow the Big Bang.

BOOMERANG

The BOOMERANG project flew instruments into Antarctica's stratosphere in balloons and mapped its microwave background using detectors cooled to a degree above absolute zero.

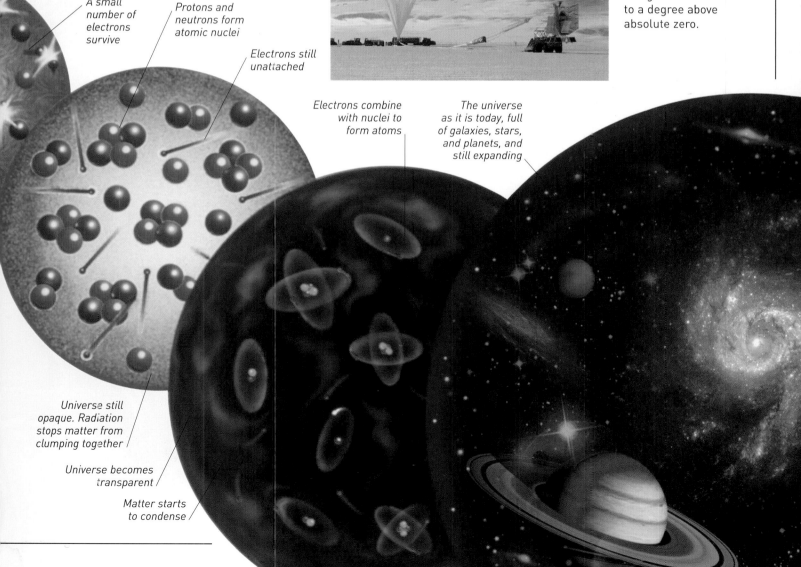

A small number of electrons survive

Protons and neutrons form atomic nuclei

Electrons still unattached

Electrons combine with nuclei to form atoms

The universe as it is today, full of galaxies, stars, and planets, and still expanding

Universe still opaque. Radiation stops matter from clumping together

Universe becomes transparent

Matter starts to condense

Fate of the universe

The Big Bang created the universe and it has been expanding ever since. But will the universe expand forever, or one day stop, and endure a long death? Or, perhaps it will shrink and squash together in a reverse Big Bang. The answer depends on the density of the universe's matter and energy, and on the effect of dark energy—an unknown gravity-opposing force.

Einstein's mistake
In 1917, when Albert Einstein described the universe mathematically, he mistakenly included a "cosmological constant," because he did not know the universe was expanding.

The expanding universe
Using the Hooker telescope (above) to study the expanding universe, Edwin Hubble discovered that the more distant a galaxy is, the faster it is traveling.

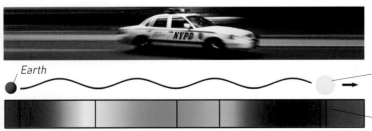

Earth

Star moving away from Earth

Spectral lines, formed by elements in a star, shift to the red

Red shifts
When a police car passes, the wavelength of its siren is stretched as it moves farther away from us. Similarly, light waves from a receding galaxy are stretched to longer (redder) wavelengths.

Universal expansion
You can imagine the expanding universe by thinking of it as a balloon with the galaxies scattered on the surface. With each blow into the balloon, the universe expands, and the galaxies move farther apart.

Galaxies were closer together in the early universe

Big Bang—origin of the universe's expansion

Distance between galaxies is increasing

Present-day universe

Universe a few billion years ago

The universe does not have a center, but from any point within it, all galaxies seem to be moving away

Universe many billions of years ago when the first galaxies formed

Galaxy structures are also evolving over time

The Big Crunch

Until the late 20th century, it was thought the universe could end in a Big Crunch. The universe collapses in a Big Crunch, where all its matter is pulled together in an infinitely small point.

New universe

Big Crunch

Big Bang

Universe expands and cools

Universe reaches maximum size

Universe collapses back on itself

New universe expands and cools forever

Dark matter

In addition to dark energy and atom-based matter, the universe is made up of 27 percent dark matter. This dark matter exists around galaxies as MACHOs (massive compact halo objects).

Gravitational lensing by dark matter

Dark particles

Weakly interacting massive particles (WIMPs) have some mass but do not interact with ordinary matter. Neutrinos might be WIMPs that make up a significant amount of dark matter.

Tracks of neutrinos in a detector

Each area of space expands slightly

Slight expansions add up to become visible over huge distances

Flying apart

Gravity is not slowing the rate of the universe's expansion, but instead accelerating it. Dark energy is causing the universe to fly apart. If its strength increases, the universe will disintegrate in a Big Rip.

Exploring Space

Astronomers have spent more than five millennia gazing at the stars, comets, planets, and moons in the heavens above us. A giant leap in astronomy came when Galileo first turned a telescope on the skies in 1609. Since then, larger telescopes have revealed a universe vaster than anyone could have imagined. Other telescopes study the invisible radiations stars and galaxies give out.

Looking with lenses

Some of the early, lens-type telescopes reached an amazing size. Christiaan Huygens' 17th century "aerial telescope" (above) was 210 ft (64 m) long.

Eyepiece

Incoming light rays

Aperture allows light to reach primary mirror

Magnetometer detects Earth's magnetic field

Light rays reflected inwards

Primary mirror

Secondary mirror bounces light to eyepiece

Light reflector

Most astronomical telescopes use a large, curved primary mirror to gather and focus light, reflecting it back along the telescope tube onto a secondary plane (flat) mirror. This mirror in turn reflects the light into an eyepiece mounted near the front of the tube.

Mounting allows accurate pointing of the telescope—this is a "Dobsonian" mount

Hubble Space Telescope

The Hubble Space Telescope (HST) is a reflector with an 8-ft (2.4-m) diameter mirror. It circles Earth every 90 minutes in an orbit about 380 miles (610 km) high. High above the atmosphere, Hubble views the universe with perfect clarity, not only at visible wavelengths but in the ultraviolet and infrared as well.

Solar arrays produce 3,000 watts of electricity

Domes of the Keck Telescopes, Mauna Kea, Hawaii

Comet Wild 2

Probing space

Stardust is a space probe that flew by Comet Wild 2 in 2004 and captured comet dust, which it returned to Earth just over two years later. Probes have been exploring space since 1959.

Stardust probe

Twin kecks

The two Keck telescopes in Hawaii have light-gathering mirrors measuring 33 ft (10 m) across, made up of 36 separate segments. Each is individually supported and computer-controlled so it always forms a perfect mirror shape.

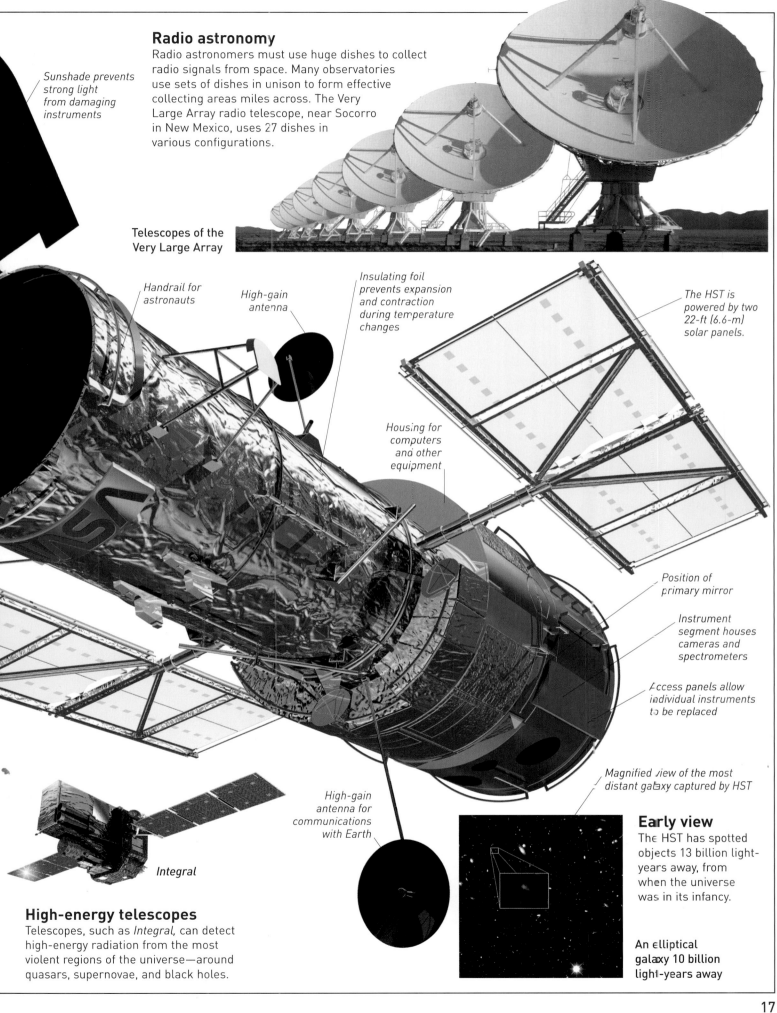

Radio astronomy

Radio astronomers must use huge dishes to collect radio signals from space. Many observatories use sets of dishes in unison to form effective collecting areas miles across. The Very Large Array radio telescope, near Socorro in New Mexico, uses 27 dishes in various configurations.

Sunshade prevents strong light from damaging instruments

Telescopes of the Very Large Array

Handrail for astronauts

High-gain antenna

Insulating foil prevents expansion and contraction during temperature changes

The HST is powered by two 22-ft (6.6-m) solar panels.

Housing for computers and other equipment

Position of primary mirror

Instrument segment houses cameras and spectrometers

Access panels allow individual instruments to be replaced

High-gain antenna for communications with Earth

Magnified view of the most distant galaxy captured by HST

Integral

High-energy telescopes

Telescopes, such as *Integral*, can detect high-energy radiation from the most violent regions of the universe—around quasars, supernovae, and black holes.

Early view

The HST has spotted objects 13 billion light-years away, from when the universe was in its infancy.

An elliptical galaxy 10 billion light-years away

Our solar system

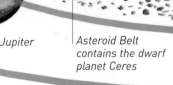

Ancient astronomers believed the Earth was the center of the universe. Today, we know the Sun is at the center of our little corner of the universe, and the Earth and planets circle that body. They are part of the Sun's family, or solar system. Eight planets, including Earth, are the most important members of the solar system, along with five dwarf planets, more than 170 moons, and billions of asteroids and comets.

Copernican system
In 1543, Polish astronomer Nicolaus Copernicus suggested that the Sun, and not Earth, was at the center of our planetary system.

Planets
A planet is a world massive enough to pull itself into a roughly spherical shape that orbits the Sun. Earth is the third planet from the Sun.

Moons
All the planets except Mercury and Venus have satellites, or moons, circling them. This is Saturn's moon, Mimas.

Mercury

Neptune takes 164.8 years to orbit the Sun

Mars takes 1.9 years to orbit the Sun

Mars

Pluto

Pluto takes 248 years to orbit the Sun once; it was classed as a planet from its discovery in 1930 until 2006

Jupiter takes 11.9 years to orbit the Sun

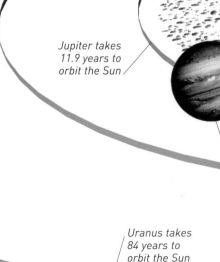

Jupiter

Asteroid Belt contains the dwarf planet Ceres

Uranus

Saturn takes 29.5 years to orbit the Sun

Dwarf planets in Kuiper Belt
Beyond Neptune is the Kuiper Belt of rock-and-ice objects, which include dwarf planets Eris (above) and Pluto.

Uranus takes 84 years to orbit the Sun

How it all began

Five billion years ago there was nothing in our corner of space but a huge billowing cloud of gas and dust. Then, after millions of years, the cloud began to collapse and spin under gravity. Over time, a thick disk of matter formed, which became progressively denser and hotter, and evolved into our Sun and then the planets.

Gas and dust collapse into disk

Central regions heat up

Sun blows away surrounding gas cloud

Planets formed as increasingly large particles came together

Asteroid Ida

Asteroids

Asteroids are lumps of rock and sometimes metal left over from the formation of the solar system. They are found mainly in a region known as the Asteroid Belt, although some asteroids stray uncomfortably close to Earth. In 1995, the probe *Galileo* photographed the 35-mile- (55-km-) long asteroid Ida on its way to Jupiter.

All eight planets follow orbits close to the plane of the Sun's equator, which is called the "plane of the ecliptic"

"We shall prove Earth to be a wandering body... and not the sink of all dull refuse of the universe."

GALILEO

Near Earth Asteroids orbit close to our planet

Sun

Venus

Earth

Neptune

Some asteroids, called Trojans, share Jupiter's orbit

Saturn

Map of the solar system

The planets orbit the Sun at different distances, from about 36 million miles (58 million km) to about 2.8 billion miles (4.5 billion km). The planets don't move in perfect circles but in elliptical (oval) orbits.

Comets

Comets are icy bodies that form a vast sphere called the Oort Cloud, which surrounds the planetary part of the solar system.

Our local star

The star we call the Sun dominates our corner of space. With a diameter of 870,000 miles (1,400,000 km), it is more than 100 times wider than Earth. The Sun is a great ball of incandescent gases that lies 93 million miles (150 million km) away from Earth. From here, it provides the light and warmth needed to give our planet life.

Sun worship
In ancient Greek mythology, the Sun god, Helios, carried the Sun across the heavens every day in a flying chariot.

Visible surface of the Sun is called the photosphere

Prominences are fountains of hot gas above the surface

The Sun's visible surface is made up of fine "granulations"

Photosphere's temperature is around 9,900°F (5,500°C)

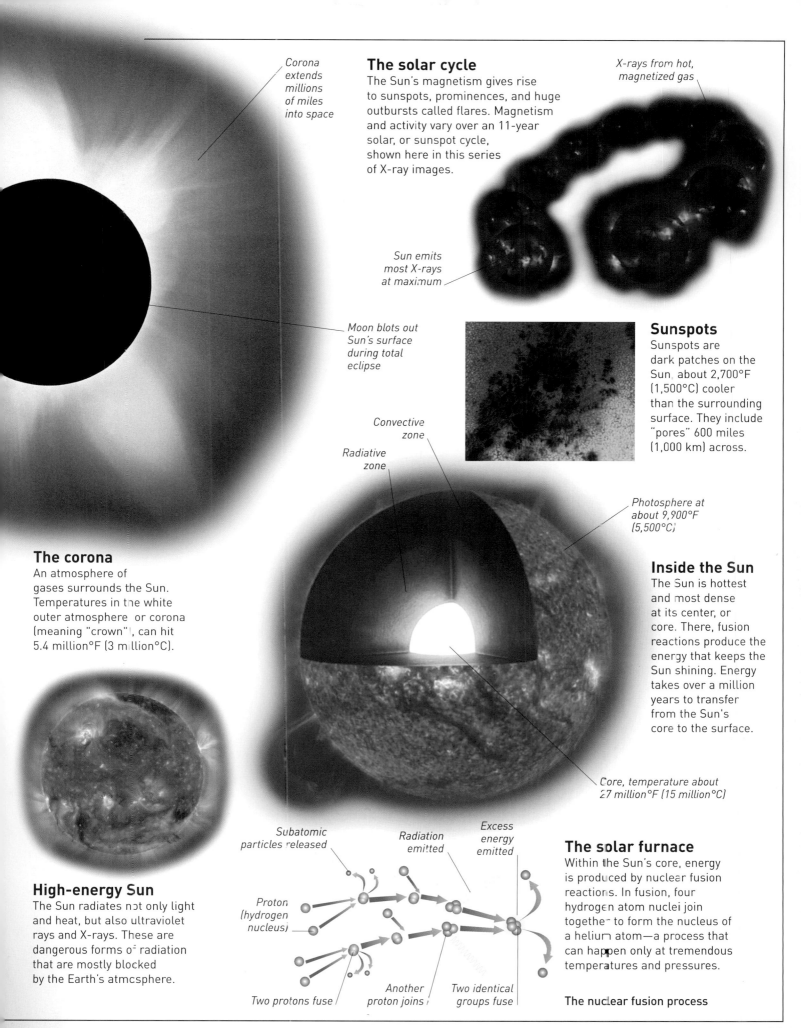

Corona extends millions of miles into space

The solar cycle
The Sun's magnetism gives rise to sunspots, prominences, and huge outbursts called flares. Magnetism and activity vary over an 11-year solar, or sunspot cycle, shown here in this series of X-ray images.

X-rays from hot, magnetized gas

Sun emits most X-rays at maximum

Moon blots out Sun's surface during total eclipse

Sunspots
Sunspots are dark patches on the Sun, about 2,700°F (1,500°C) cooler than the surrounding surface. They include "pores" 600 miles (1,000 km) across.

Convective zone

Radiative zone

Photosphere at about 9,900°F (5,500°C)

The corona
An atmosphere of gases surrounds the Sun. Temperatures in the white outer atmosphere or corona (meaning "crown"), can hit 5.4 million°F (3 million°C).

Inside the Sun
The Sun is hottest and most dense at its center, or core. There, fusion reactions produce the energy that keeps the Sun shining. Energy takes over a million years to transfer from the Sun's core to the surface.

Core, temperature about 27 million°F (15 million°C)

Subatomic particles released

Radiation emitted

Excess energy emitted

Proton (hydrogen nucleus)

The solar furnace
Within the Sun's core, energy is produced by nuclear fusion reactions. In fusion, four hydrogen atom nuclei join together to form the nucleus of a helium atom—a process that can happen only at tremendous temperatures and pressures.

High-energy Sun
The Sun radiates not only light and heat, but also ultraviolet rays and X-rays. These are dangerous forms of radiation that are mostly blocked by the Earth's atmosphere.

Two protons fuse

Another proton joins

Two identical groups fuse

The nuclear fusion process

Earth's Moon

The Moon is Earth's closest companion in space and its only natural satellite. On average, it lies 239,000 miles (384,000 km) away. It has no light of its own, but shines by reflecting sunlight. As the Moon circles the Earth, it appears to change shape, from a slim crescent to full circle, and back again every 29.5 days. With a diameter of 2,160 miles (3,476 km), the Moon is a rocky world like Earth, but has no atmosphere, water, or life.

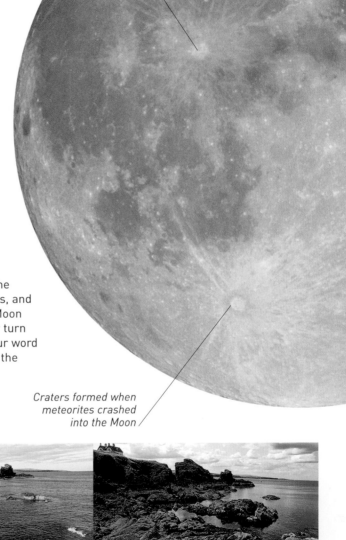

Bright crater surrounded by rays

Craters formed when meteorites crashed into the Moon

New Moon

Crescent

The dark part of the crescent Moon sometimes reflects light from Earth

First quarter

Waxing gibbous

Full Moon

Waning gibbous

Last quarter

Decrescent

Actor Lon Chaney Jr. in **The Wolf Man** *(1941)*

Lunar legends

Ancient people thought the Moon had magical powers, and that the light of the full Moon could make them mad or turn them into werewolves. Our word lunatic comes from *luna*, the Latin word for the Moon.

The changing face

The changing phases of the Moon happen as the Sun lights up different amounts of the side that faces Earth. At new Moon, we can't see it because the Sun is lighting up only the far side. As the Moon moves around in its orbit, more and more of its face gets lit up.

Lunar gravity

The Moon's gravity is only one-sixth of Earth's, so it cannot retain any gases to make an atmosphere. The lack of atmosphere means the temperature varies from 230°F (110°C) to -290°F (-180°C). Weak though it is, the Moon's gravity still affects Earth. It tugs at the oceans to create tides.

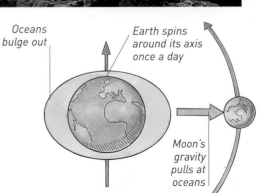

Oceans bulge out

Earth spins around its axis once a day

Moon's gravity pulls at oceans

The face of the Moon

The Moon always presents the same face toward Earth. This happens because it spins once on its axis in exactly the same time as it circles once around Earth—27.3 days. This motion is called captured rotation. The dark regions we see on the Moon's face are vast dusty plains, although early astronomers thought they might be seas.

Walking on the Moon

In 1969, *Apollo 11* astronauts Neil Armstrong and Buzz Aldrin planted the first human footprints on the Moon. They were the first of 12 US astronauts to explore the surface, set up scientific stations, and collect samples of soil and rock.

Aitken Basin is the largest crater on the Moon

The Moon's south polar region

The hidden poles

Space probes have shown that some polar craters could contain deposits of ice. If proven, this ice could provide water for future human explorers.

The far side

No one had seen the Moon's far side until the first blurred images of it were taken in 1959. It is more rugged than the nearside, and has no large "seas."

Dark maria (seas) are plains of solidified lava

Lunar highlands

The Earth seen from above the Moon

Lunar surface many miles below

Earthrise

The *Apollo* astronauts took stunning photographs of the Moon, including dramatic shots of the Earth rising over the Moon's horizon. These showed the contrast between our colorful, living world and its drab, dead satellite.

Comparing the planets

Going out from the Sun, the eight planets are Mercury, Venus, Earth, Mars, Jupiter, Saturn, Uranus, and Neptune. The four small inner planets are made up mainly of rock, and the four giant outer ones are made up mainly of gas. Each planet orbits the Sun and also spins on its own axis.

The planets to scale

The planets vary widely in size. Jupiter contains more matter than all the other planets put together. It could swallow more than 25,000 worlds the size of Mercury. Mercury, by comparison, is tiny—Jupiter has a moon bigger than Mercury.

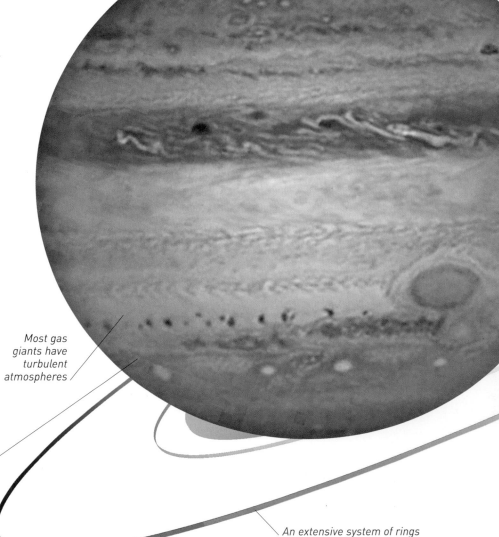

MERCURY
Diameter: 3,032 miles/4,880 km
Distance from Sun: 36 million miles/ 58 million km
Rotation period: 58.7 days
Time to orbit Sun: 88 days
No. of moons: 0

EARTH
Diameter: 7,926 miles/12,756 km
Distance from Sun: 93 million miles/ 149.6 million km
Rotation period: 23.93 hours
Time to orbit Sun: 365.25 days
No. of moons: 1

VENUS
Diameter: 7,521 miles/ 12,104 km
Distance from Sun: 67 million miles/ 108 million km
Rotation period: 243 days
Time to orbit Sun: 224.7 days
No. of moons: 0

MARS
Diameter: 4,222 miles/ 6,794 km
Distance from Sun: 142 million miles/ 228 million km
Rotation period: 24.6 hours
Time to orbit Sun: 687 days
No. of moons: 2

Most gas giants have turbulent atmospheres

JUPITER
Diameter: 88,846 miles/142,984 km
Distance from Sun: 484 million miles/778 million km
Rotation period: 9.93 hours
Time to orbit Sun: 11.9 years
No. of moons: 67

An extensive system of rings surrounds Saturn's equator, spanning a distance of more than 250,000 miles (400,000 km) out from the edge of the planet. All four gas giants have ring systems

Orbits to scale

The diagram below shows the distances of the planets from the Sun (to scale). The inner planets are close together, the outer planets far apart.

Mercury

Earth

Venus Mars

Jupiter

Saturn

In the ecliptic

The planets circle the Sun close to a flat plane called the "plane of the ecliptic." In Earth's skies, the ecliptic is the path the Sun appears to take through the heavens during a year.

The five naked-eye planets aligned along the ecliptic

SATURN
Diameter: 74,900 miles/
120,536 km
Distance from Sun:
890 million miles/
1,433 million km
Rotation period: 10.66 hours
Time to orbit Sun: 29.5 years
No. of moons: 62

As shown by the tilt of Saturn's rings, planets do not orbit the Sun bolt upright—most are tilted over to some extent

URANUS
Diameter: 31,770 miles/
51,118 km
Distance from Sun:
1.79 billion miles/
2.87 billion km
Rotation period: 17.24 hours
Time to orbit Sun: 84 years
No. of moons: 27

NEPTUNE
Diameter: 30,780 miles/49,532 km
Distance from Sun: 2.78 billion miles/4.49 billion km
Rotation period: 16.11 hours
Time to orbit Sun: 164.8 years
No. of moons: 14

Gas giants

The four planets from Jupiter to Neptune are gas giants. They have an atmosphere of mainly hydrogen and helium, with a planet-wide ocean of slushy ice or liquid hydrogen underneath. At the center is a small core of rock.

Outer atmosphere

Liquid hydrogen molecules

Structure of Jupiter

Liquid atomic hydrogen

Core

Mantle *Core*

Crust

Atmosphere

Structure of Mars

Rocky planets

The four inner planets, from Mercury to Mars, have a rocky structure. They have a thin, hard outer crust, which overlays another thicker layer, called the mantle. In the center is a core of metal, mainly iron.

Uranus

Neptune

Rocky worlds

Two rocky planets, Mercury and Venus, orbit closer to the Sun than Earth. Both planets are hotter than Earth—surface temperatures on Mercury rise as high as 840°F (450°C), and on Venus, up to 86°F (30°C) higher. But the two are very different. Mercury has no appreciable atmosphere, whereas Venus's dense atmosphere stops us from seeing the surface.

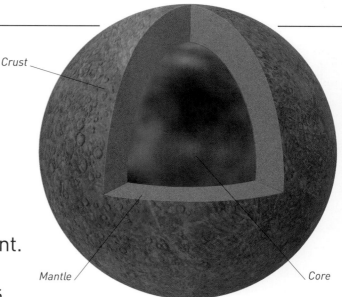

Crust

Mantle

Core

Inside Mercury
Mercury is a small planet, with a diameter of 3,032 miles (4,880 km). Like Earth, Mercury is made up of a hard outer crust, a rocky mantle, and an iron core.

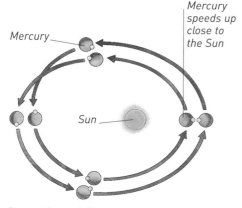

Mercury

Mercury speeds up close to the Sun

Sun

Speedy orbit
Mercury orbits the Sun in just 88 days, but rotates only once every 59 days. This means Mercury rotates three times every two orbits (as shown above).

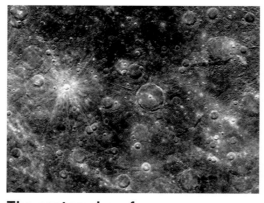

The cratered surface
Mercury was bombarded with meteorites billions of years ago, resulting in the cratered, landscape we see today. Caloris Basin is one such crater 800 miles (1,300 km) across.

Clouds of sulfuric acid

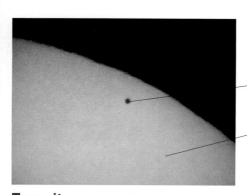

Mercury

Sun's surface

Transits
Mercury and Venus circle the Sun inside Earth's orbit and sometimes pass in front of the Sun as seen from Earth. We call these rare crossings, transits.

Cook's tour
In 1768, Britain's Royal Society sent James Cook on the first scientific expedition to the Pacific Ocean. In Tahiti, Cook recorded the transit of Venus, which was used to measure the distance from Earth to the Sun. Cook later sailed his ship *Endeavour* to New Zealand and Australia.

Earth's deadly twin

Venus and Earth are almost identical in size but are very different worlds. Venus is a hostile planet, with high temperatures, a crushing atmosphere of carbon dioxide, and clouds made up of droplets of sulfuric acid. No human could survive there for even a minute.

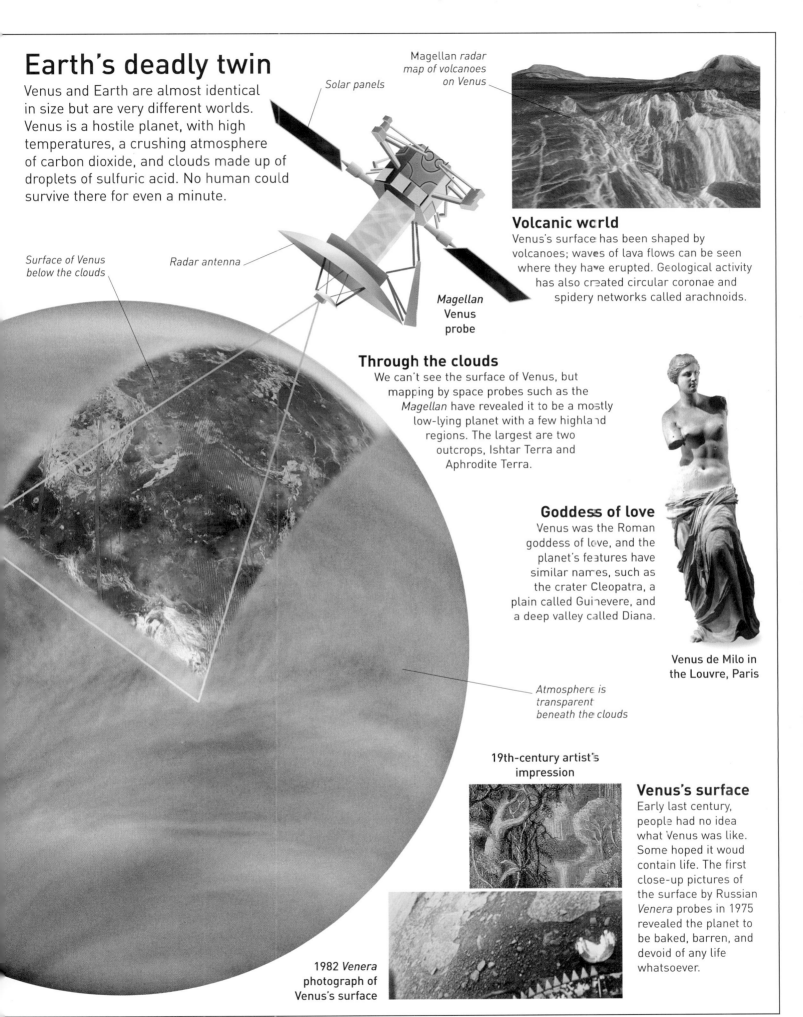

Solar panels

Magellan radar map of volcanoes on Venus

Surface of Venus below the clouds

Radar antenna

Magellan Venus probe

Volcanic world

Venus's surface has been shaped by volcanoes; waves of lava flows can be seen where they have erupted. Geological activity has also created circular coronae and spidery networks called arachnoids.

Through the clouds

We can't see the surface of Venus, but mapping by space probes such as the *Magellan* have revealed it to be a mostly low-lying planet with a few highland regions. The largest are two outcrops, Ishtar Terra and Aphrodite Terra.

Goddess of love

Venus was the Roman goddess of love, and the planet's features have similar names, such as the crater Cleopatra, a plain called Guinevere, and a deep valley called Diana.

Venus de Milo in the Louvre, Paris

Atmosphere is transparent beneath the clouds

19th-century artist's impression

Venus's surface

Early last century, people had no idea what Venus was like. Some hoped it woud contain life. The first close-up pictures of the surface by Russian *Venera* probes in 1975 revealed the planet to be baked, barren, and devoid of any life whatsoever.

1982 *Venera* photograph of Venus's surface

Home planet

With a diameter of 7,926 miles (12,756 km), Earth is Venus's near twin in size, but the similarity ends there. At 93 million miles (150 million km) from the Sun, Earth is not a hellish place like Venus, but a haven for life. It is a rocky planet, but its surface is made up of plates instead of being solid.

Earth god
The ancient Egyptians believed in many sky gods, including Nut, who is shown here held aloft by Shu. The Earth god Geb reclines on the ground.

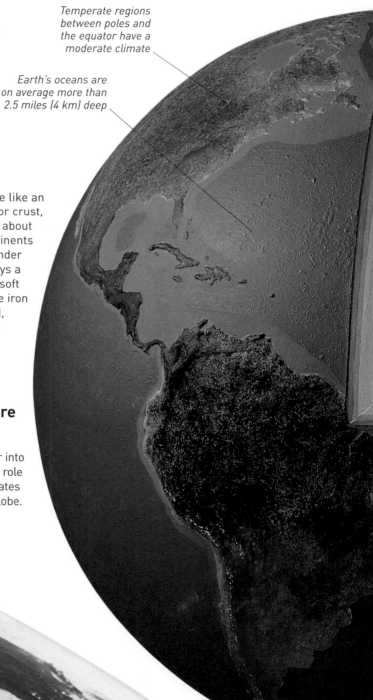

Temperate regions between poles and the equator have a moderate climate

Earth's oceans are on average more than 2.5 miles (4 km) deep

Plate tectonics
The study of Earth's shifting crust is called plate tectonics. Often, colliding plates destroy rocks and create volcanoes.

Inside Earth
Earth has a layered structure like an onion. It has an outer layer, or crust, of thin, hard rock, averaging about 25 miles (40 km) on the continents and about 6 miles (10 km) under the oceans. The crust overlays a heavier rocky mantle with a soft top. Deeper down lies a huge iron core. The outer core is liquid, while the inner core is solid.

Oceans and atmosphere
Oceans cover more than 70 percent of Earth's surface. The evaporation of ocean water into the atmosphere plays a crucial role in the planet's climate and dictates weather patterns around the globe.

Earth seen from orbit

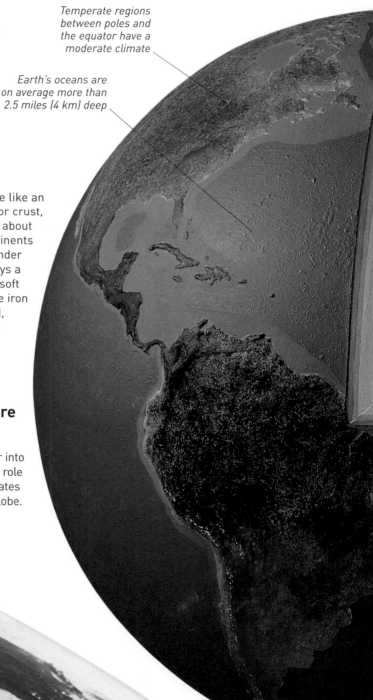

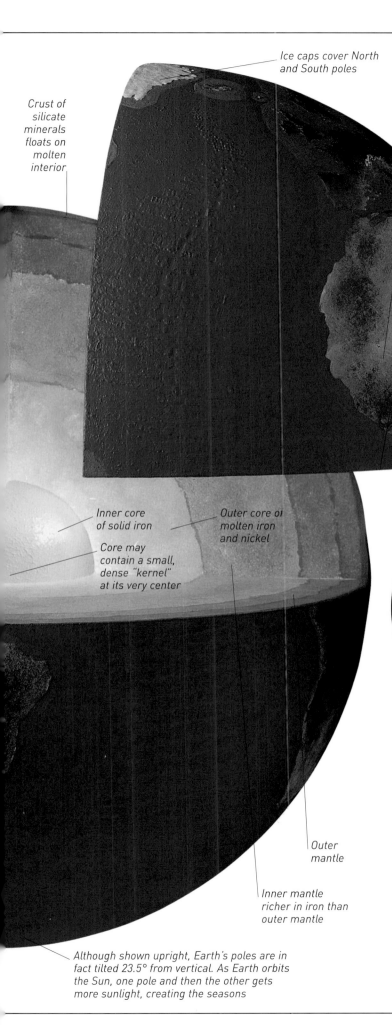

Crust of silicate minerals floats on molten interior

Ice caps cover North and South poles

Arid desert regions lie close to the equator

Earth bulges at the equator—its diameter here is 13 miles (21 km) more than at the poles

Inner core of solid iron

Outer core of molten iron and nickel

Core may contain a small, dense "kernel" at its very center

Outer mantle

Inner mantle richer in iron than outer mantle

Although shown upright, Earth's poles are in fact tilted 23.5° from vertical. As Earth orbits the Sun, one pole and then the other gets more sunlight, creating the seasons

Antarctica

Death Valley, California

Climate extremes

Antarctica recorded the lowest ever temperature of -135.8°F (-94.7°C), while temperatures often hit 122°F (50°C) in California's Death Valley.

The magnetic shield

Earth's magnetism creates the magnetosphere—a cocoon around the Earth that shields it against the Sun's deadly radiation. It also sometimes traps particles that create the beautiful light displays we call the aurorae.

Aurorae photographed from the Space Shuttle

Life in abundance

With comfortable temperatures, liquid water, and oxygen in the atmosphere, Earth can support an amazing variety of life. This includes primitive microscopic organisms such as viruses, to towering redwood trees and intelligent mammals, like ourselves.

Life thriving on and around a coral reef

Mars, the Red Planet

The reddish hue of Mars makes it a distinctive member of our solar system. With a diameter of 4,222 miles (6,794 km), Mars is about half the size of Earth, and its day is only about half an hour longer than our own. It also has seasons, an atmosphere, and ice caps at the poles. But Mars's thin atmosphere and barren surface are not suitable for life.

Northern half of Mars is mostly low-lying plains

Valles Marineris canyon system is 4 miles (6 km) deep in places

Southern hemisphere is dominated by Moon-like, cratered highlands

A wet world?
Ancient floodplains and dry riverbeds are evidence that water flowed across Mars billions of years ago. Water still exists on Mars in ice caps, shown on the map above in deep blue.

Exploring the surface

The surface of Mars has been more extensively explored than that of any planet other than Earth. Craft have photographed its landscape from orbit and landing probes have taken close-up pictures of its surface. The latest rover to explore the Martian surface is *Curiosity*, which arrived in 2012.

Phobos

Deimos

Dogs of war

Mars has two tiny moons, Phobos and Deimos. Phobos measures about 16 miles (26 km) across and Deimos, just 10 miles (16 km) across.

Rockstrewn landscape of Ares Vallis region

Sojourner *rover*

On top of the world

Olympus Mons is the largest of four volcanoes near Mars's equator. It is 15 miles (24 km) high—nearly three times higher than Mount Everest—and has a crater 55 miles (90 km) wide. It last erupted about 25 million years ago.

Martian weather

Strong Martian winds reaching 185 mph (300 kph) often whip up surface dust to create dust devils (above) and massive dust storms.

Deadly heat ray

Martian war machine

Martians are coming

Thoughts of a Martian race fighting to survive in a hostile climate, stimulated the imagination of English author H. G. Wells. In 1898, he published a groundbreaking science fiction novel *The War of the Worlds*, which featured a Martian invasion of Earth.

1907 illustration from *The War of the Worlds*

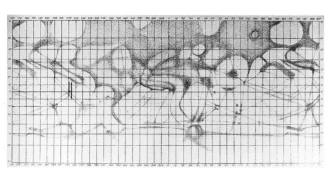

The canals of Mars

Italian astronomer Giovanni Schiaparelli first reported seeing channels on Mars in 1877. An optical illusion, these channels made astronomers think a Martian race was digging canals.

King of the planets

More massive than all the other planets put together, Jupiter is the largest member of the solar system after the Sun. One of the gas giants, Jupiter has an atmosphere of hydrogen and helium above an ocean of liquid hydrogen. Dark and pale belts and zones cross Jupiter's face. These are clouds that have been drawn out by the planet's rapid rotation; Jupiter spins around once in less than 10 hours.

Ruler of the gods
Jupiter is an appropriate name for the king of the planets, because Jupiter was the king of the gods in Roman mythology. The ancient Greeks called him Zeus.

Antenna sends data back to Earth and receives instructions

Heat from nuclear fuel powers the spacecraft

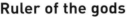

Science instruments

Galileo
The space probe *Galileo* reached Jupiter in 1995 after a five-year journey through space. *Galileo* confirmed that the top layer of Jupiter's clouds consists of ammonia ice; it detected winds in the atmosphere reaching 400 mph (650 kph).

Earth to same scale

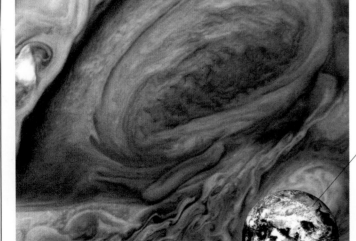

Great Red Spot
Jupiter's Great Red Spot is a super hurricane, with winds swirling around at high speeds. The Spot towers 5 miles (8 km) above the surrounding cloud as the swirling currents rise. It changes in size, but averages about 25,000 miles (40,000 km) across.

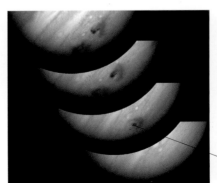

Target Jupiter
In 1994, fragments of Comet Shoemaker-Levy 9 smashed into Jupiter after the planet had disrupted the comet's orbit. The impacts created huge fireballs.

The plume (bottom) and the developing scar made by the impact of a comet fragment

Io

The colorful moon Io is covered with sulfur flows from its many volcanoes. Volcanic eruptions also shoot plumes of gas 150 miles (250 km) above Io's surface.

Sulfur-covered surface

Volcanic eruption on Io

Europa

Europa has a network of grooves and ridges that crisscross its icy surface. Some astronomers think a liquid ocean could lie beneath the ice.

Europa's surface reflects light well

Cracks in Europa's surface ice

Ganymede

Ganymede, diameter 3,273 miles (5,268 km), is the biggest moon in the solar system. Ganymede has an old icy surface, with dark areas and paler grooved regions. Recent craters show up white, where fresh ice has been exposed.

Light areas seem to show where ice has welled up from inside Ganymede

Dark regions of older surface

Callisto

Callisto orbits farther out than Ganymede and looks quite different, being almost completely covered with craters. Its crust is thought to date back billions of years.

Dark surface

Bright craters reveal fresh ice below surface

Galileo's moons

Italian astronomer Galileo Galilei was among the first to observe the heavens through a telescope (above) in 1609. He saw mountains on the Moon, sunspots, and Venus's phases. He also saw Jupiter's four biggest moons, now called "Galilean" moons.

Ringed Saturn

Saturn is a favorite planet because of the glorious system of shining rings that circles its equator. Saturn is the sixth planet from the Sun and the second largest after Jupiter, measuring 74,900 miles (120,536 km) across. Saturn is made up mainly of hydrogen and helium around a rocky core, like Jupiter, but is even less dense. Indeed, Saturn is so light that it would float in water.

The ring cycle
Saturn's axis is tilted at an angle of nearly 27 degrees, which enables us to see its rings at various angles during its journey around the Sun.

B ring

Shadow cast by Saturn across rings

F ring

Inside the rings
Saturn's rings are made up of thousands of narrow ringlets formed from chunks of dirty water ice whizzing around in orbit at high speed.

Ring world
Through Earth-based telescopes, astronomers can see three rings around Saturn—the A, B, and C rings. The broadest and brightest ring is the B ring, while the faintest is the C ring (also called the Crepe ring). The B ring is separated from the A ring by the Cassini Division, and there is a smaller gap, called the Encke Division, near the outer edge of the A ring.

Shadow of rings on planet

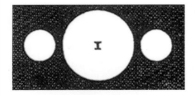
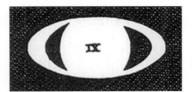

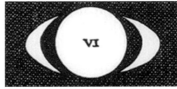

Mystery planet
In his book *Systema Saturnium,* Christiaan Huygens examined drawings of Saturn by astronomers such as Galileo (above) and concluded that the planet was surrounded by a thin, flat ring.

Giovanni Cassini
Late 17th-century astronomers believed that Saturn's rings must be solid or liquid. But doubts emerged in 1675, when astronomer Giovanni Domenico Cassini discovered a dark line in Saturn's ring. This was a gap between two rings, now known as the Cassini Division. Cassini realized then that the rings couldn't be solid.

Storm world
The bands in Saturn's atmosphere are streams of gases coursing around the planet at high speeds and in opposite directions, creating storms.

Saturn's rapid rotation makes it bulge out at the equator

D ring

C ring

B ring

Cassini division

Icy surface
With a diameter of about 300 miles (500 km), Enceladus is the sixth largest of Saturn's 62 moons. It has an icy surface that is mostly smooth, but cratered and crisscrossed in parts.

Inner A ring

Encke division

Outer A ring

Thick orange clouds obscure Titan's surface

Planet-sized Titan
With a diameter of 3,200 miles (5,150 km), Saturn's largest moon, Titan, is bigger than Mercury and second only to Jupiter's Ganymede.

Infrared map of Titan's surface

Under the clouds
Titan's atmosphere is mainly hydrogen, with traces of other gases, including methane. In 2005, the *Huygens* space probe descended to Titan's surface and recorded riverlike features there.

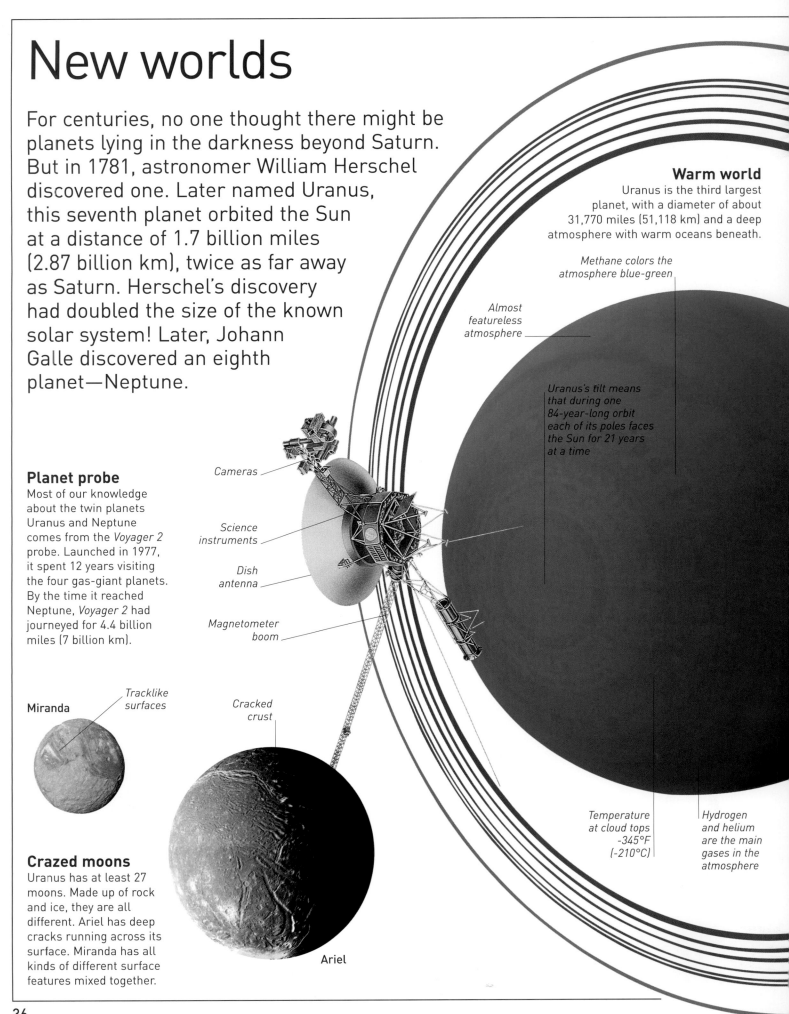

New worlds

For centuries, no one thought there might be planets lying in the darkness beyond Saturn. But in 1781, astronomer William Herschel discovered one. Later named Uranus, this seventh planet orbited the Sun at a distance of 1.7 billion miles (2.87 billion km), twice as far away as Saturn. Herschel's discovery had doubled the size of the known solar system! Later, Johann Galle discovered an eighth planet—Neptune.

Warm world
Uranus is the third largest planet, with a diameter of about 31,770 miles (51,118 km) and a deep atmosphere with warm oceans beneath.

Methane colors the atmosphere blue-green

Almost featureless atmosphere

Uranus's tilt means that during one 84-year-long orbit each of its poles faces the Sun for 21 years at a time

Planet probe
Most of our knowledge about the twin planets Uranus and Neptune comes from the *Voyager 2* probe. Launched in 1977, it spent 12 years visiting the four gas-giant planets. By the time it reached Neptune, *Voyager 2* had journeyed for 4.4 billion miles (7 billion km).

Cameras

Science instruments

Dish antenna

Magnetometer boom

Tracklike surfaces

Miranda

Cracked crust

Crazed moons
Uranus has at least 27 moons. Made up of rock and ice, they are all different. Ariel has deep cracks running across its surface. Miranda has all kinds of different surface features mixed together.

Ariel

Temperature at cloud tops -345°F (-210°C)

Hydrogen and helium are the main gases in the atmosphere

Blue planet

Neptune lies 1 billion miles (1.6 billion km) beyond Uranus. It is slightly smaller than its neighbor, with a diameter of 30,780 miles (49,532 km), and has a fainter ring system. The atmosphere is flecked with bright clouds and sometimes with dark storm regions. It is bluer than Uranus because it contains more methane.

Dark spots are lower in atmosphere than bright, high-speed "scooters"

Cloud temperature -345°F (-210°C)

Triton's geysers

Triton is the largest of Neptune's 14 moons, 1,680 miles (2,710 km) across. It is a deep-frozen world, covered with frozen nitrogen and methane, and has geysers erupting on it. The geysers spurt out nitrogen gas and dust.

Neptune find

Johann Galle first observed Neptune in 1846, after French mathematician Urbain Leverrier had calculated where it should be found.

REPUBLIQUE FRANÇAISE
POSTES
12F
1811 LE VERRIER 1877

Uranus has a total of 13 rings around its equator

Ring particles average about 3 ft (1 m) across

The moon Charon circles around Pluto every six days

Outer ring is brightest

Icy outcasts

Pluto has been classed as a dwarf planet since 2006. It is smaller than Earth's Moon, measuring only 1,413 miles (2,274 km) across, and it has five moons of its own. Pluto is made up of rock and ice, with frozen nitrogen and methane covering its surface.

Pluto lies, on average, 3,670 million miles (5,900 million km) from the Sun

Asteroids and meteors

The solar system has many members besides planets, dwarf planets, and moons. Rocky asteroids orbit close to the Sun while smaller icy bodies lurk at the solar system's edge. Those traveling in toward the Sun release clouds of gas and dust and become comets (see p. 40). Asteroid and comet particles are called meteoroids. When they enter Earth's atmosphere, most burn up as meteors, also called shooting stars.

Asteroid Ida

The Asteroid Belt
About 400,000 individual asteroids have been identified, but there are billions altogether. Most of them circle the Sun in a broad band called the Asteroid Belt.

Asteroid variety
Even the largest asteroid, Ceres, is only 580 miles (930 km) across, making it less than one-third the size of the Moon. The next largest, Pallas and Vesta, are only about half the size of Ceres. But most asteroids are much smaller—Gaspra, for example, is only about 11 miles (18 km) long. Gaspra, like many asteroids, is mostly made up of silicate rocks.

The celestial police
In 1800, Baron Franz von Zach organized some "Celestial Police" astronomers to look for a planet in the "gap" in the solar system between Mars and Jupiter. They were upstaged by Giuseppe Piazzi, who spotted the dwarf planet Ceres in the gap.

Giuseppe Piazzi
(1746–1826)

Asteroid mining
The metallic asteroids are rich in iron, as well as nickel and other metals that are comparatively rare on Earth. Metals in asteroids exist in pure form, not in ores as on Earth, and this makes them much easier to extract. In the future, humans may mine the asteroids.

Eros

NEAR-
Shoemaker
spacecraft

Near Eros

In 2001, the probe *NEAR-Shoemaker*
performed a remarkable feat. It landed
on the asteroid Eros, a rocky lump
only about 20 miles (33 km) long.

Meteor shower

The streaks of light
we see in the night sky
are meteors. They are
produced by meteoroid
particles little bigger
than sand grains. As
they move through
the atmosphere, the
particles cause the
gas atoms in the
atmosphere to glow.

The 1833 Leonid
meteor storm over
Niagara Falls

*Ida's deeply gouged
surface probably formed
as it broke up from a
larger asteroid millions
of years ago*

*Meteorites
stand out in a
rockless
landscape*

*NASA's Nomad robot
locates meteorites in
Antarctica*

Looking for meteorites

Antarctica has provided rich pickings for hunters
of meteorites—meteoroid lumps that have
survived passage through the atmosphere.

*Gaspra has fewer
craters than Ida—it
probably also formed
in a breakup*

Asteroid
Gaspra

Micrograph showing crystals in
a stony meteorite.

Stone and metal

Most of the meteorites
that have been recovered
are made up of stony
material. But all of the
biggest ones are made up of
metal, mainly iron and nickel.

*Crater rim is filled
with a lake now used
as a reservoir*

*Crater floor may
hide huge nickel
deposits*

Manicouagan
crater, Quebec

Impact
craters

From time to time,
really big meteorites
smash into Earth's surface
and gouge out large craters.
Around 200 million years ago,
a meteorite created this crater in
Canada, which has since filled with ice.

Icy wanderers

In the outer reaches of the solar system, there are huge chunks of icy debris. Each of these is the city-sized nucleus of a comet; a dirty snowball that remains invisible unless it travels toward the Sun and is heated. It then develops a large head and tails. At their brightest, comets can rival the brightest planets, and can develop tails that stretch for millions of miles.

Happy returns
In his painting, *Adoration of the Magi*, Giotto included a comet based on one he had seen in 1301. Giotto's comet was Halley's Comet, whose orbit brings it close to the Sun once every 76 years.

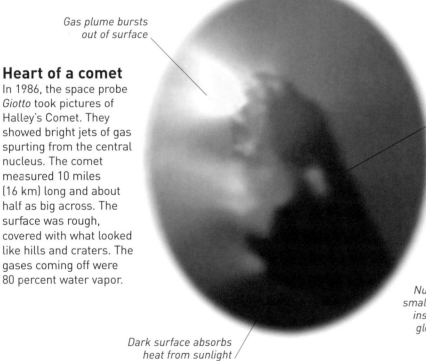

Gas plume bursts out of surface

Heart of a comet
In 1986, the space probe *Giotto* took pictures of Halley's Comet. They showed bright jets of gas spurting from the central nucleus. The comet measured 10 miles (16 km) long and about half as big across. The surface was rough, covered with what looked like hills and craters. The gases coming off were 80 percent water vapor.

Dark surface absorbs heat from sunlight

Straight gas tail streams away, driven by solar wind

Dark dust coats nucleus

Gas tail glows as solar wind strikes gas from comet

Nucleus is too small to be seen inside comet's glowing coma

Fragile snowballs
Like snowballs, comets are not firmly held together and often break up. In 1992, a comet passed close to Jupiter and was ripped apart by the giant planet's gravity. The fragmented comet, called Shoemaker-Levy 9, collided with Jupiter two years later.

Comet of the century
In 1997, Earth's sky was dominated by one of the brightest comets of the 20th century. Comet Hale-Bopp outshone all but the brightest stars and hung in the night sky for weeks. It had two well-developed tails streaming away from the bright head, or coma. There was a curved, yellowish dust tail and a straighter blue gas, or ion, tail.

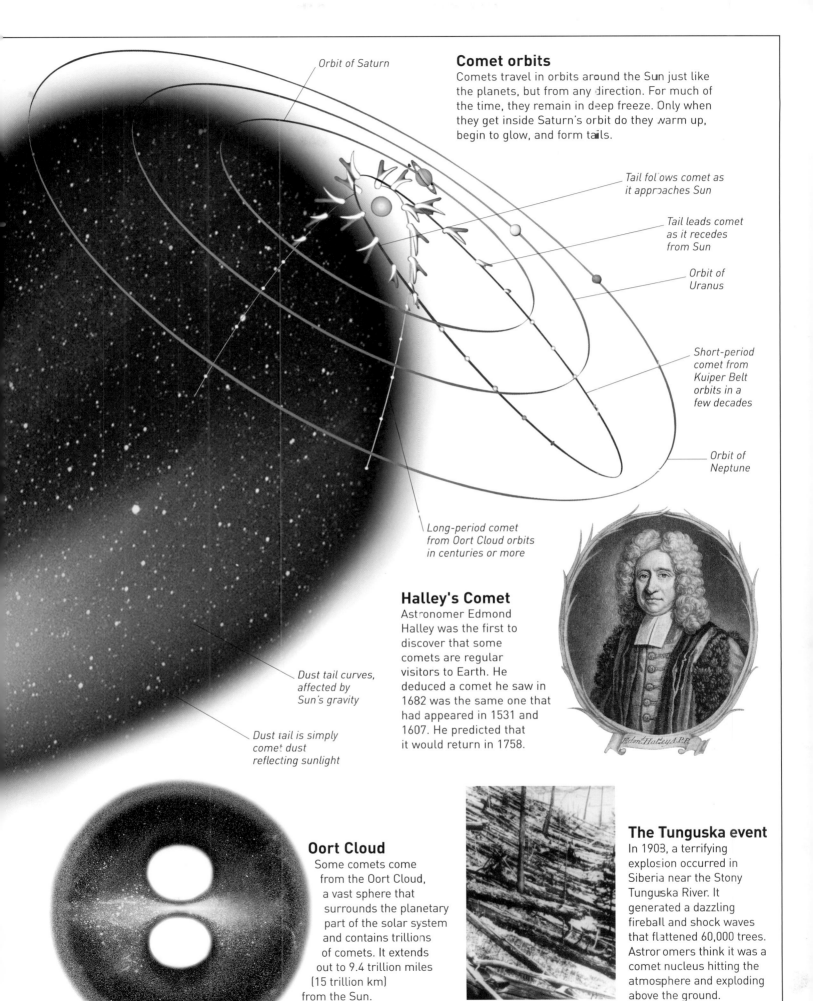

Comet orbits

Comets travel in orbits around the Sun just like the planets, but from any direction. For much of the time, they remain in deep freeze. Only when they get inside Saturn's orbit do they warm up, begin to glow, and form tails.

Orbit of Saturn

Tail follows comet as it approaches Sun

Tail leads comet as it recedes from Sun

Orbit of Uranus

Short-period comet from Kuiper Belt orbits in a few decades

Orbit of Neptune

Long-period comet from Oort Cloud orbits in centuries or more

Dust tail curves, affected by Sun's gravity

Dust tail is simply comet dust reflecting sunlight

Halley's Comet

Astronomer Edmond Halley was the first to discover that some comets are regular visitors to Earth. He deduced a comet he saw in 1682 was the same one that had appeared in 1531 and 1607. He predicted that it would return in 1758.

Edm.Halley A.P.R.

Oort Cloud

Some comets come from the Oort Cloud, a vast sphere that surrounds the planetary part of the solar system and contains trillions of comets. It extends out to 9.4 trillion miles (15 trillion km) from the Sun.

The Tunguska event

In 1908, a terrifying explosion occurred in Siberia near the Stony Tunguska River. It generated a dazzling fireball and shock waves that flattened 60,000 trees. Astronomers think it was a comet nucleus hitting the atmosphere and exploding above the ground.

41

Distant suns

Every clear night you could probably count as many as 2,500 stars in the sky. They always appear as tiny pinpricks of light, but they are actually huge, bright bodies like the Sun. However, even the closest star to the Sun—Proxima Centauri—lies more than four light-years away from Earth.

A universe of stars

In the Milky Way, stars appear crammed together in their millions. Each star has a different brightness, color, size, and mass. There are around 500 billion in our galaxy alone.

Stars of the Sagittarius Star Cloud

Star Cloud lies 25,000 light-years from Earth, toward the center of the Milky Way

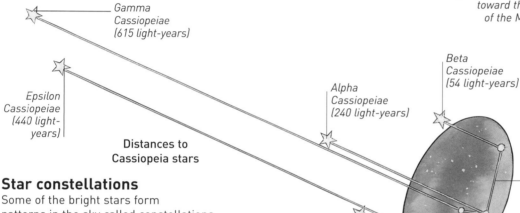

Gamma Cassiopeiae (615 light-years)

Epsilon Cassiopeiae (440 light-years)

Distances to Cassiopeia stars

Alpha Cassiopeiae (240 light-years)

Beta Cassiopeiae (54 light-years)

Star pattern in the constellation Cassiopeia

Delta Cassiopeiae (100 light-years)

Star constellations

Some of the bright stars form patterns in the sky called constellations. Ancient astronomers named them after figures from their myths and legends. The constellation stars look the same distance from Earth, but that is only because they lie in the same direction.

How far away?

The distance to the nearest stars can be measured by the parallax method. Astronomers use the method by viewing a nearby star first from one side of Earth's orbit, then from the other. They measure the amount a star appears to move against more distant stars, to calculate its distance.

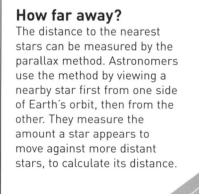

Distant stars

Closer star B has larger parallax shift than more distant star A

A

B

Parallax shift against distant background stars

Line of sight to star B

Line of sight to star A

Earth's position in January

Earth's position in July

Sun

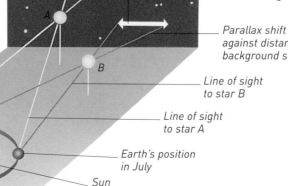

Betelgeuse (magnitude 0.8)

Betelgeuse and Rigel seem the same brightness, but Rigel is farther away

Rigel (magnitude 0.1)

Star brightness

The stars in constellations differ in brightness, as seen here in Orion. We measure brightness on a scale introduced by astronomer Hipparchus, more than 2,000 years ago. He graded the brightest stars as first-magnitude stars, and the dimmest ones as sixth-magnitude.

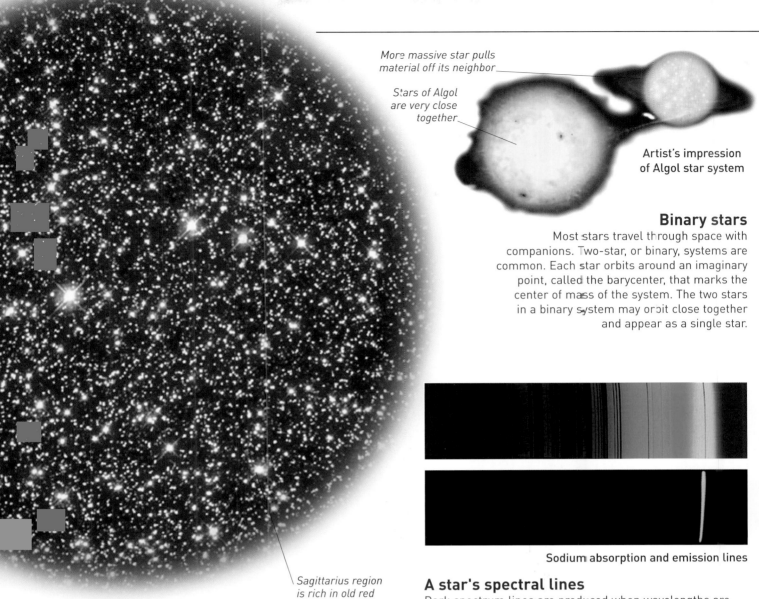

More massive star pulls material off its neighbor

Stars of Algol are very close together

Artist's impression of Algol star system

Binary stars

Most stars travel through space with companions. Two-star, or binary, systems are common. Each star orbits around an imaginary point, called the barycenter, that marks the center of mass of the system. The two stars in a binary system may orbit close together and appear as a single star.

Sodium absorption and emission lines

A star's spectral lines

Dark spectrum lines are produced when wavelengths are removed. Sodium removes yellow wavelengths (top) and emits the same lengths when hot (below).

Sagittarius region is rich in old red and yellow stars

Spectroscopy

The white light we receive from the stars is made up of different colors, or wavelengths. Using a spectroscope, we can split starlight into its separate colors to form a rainbowlike spectrum. Dark lines cross the spectrum at intervals.

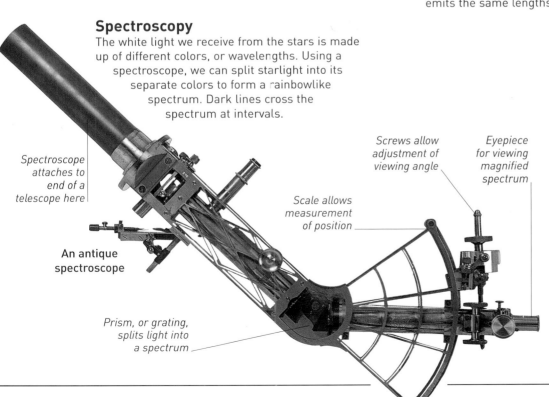

Spectroscope attaches to end of a telescope here

Screws allow adjustment of viewing angle

Eyepiece for viewing magnified spectrum

Scale allows measurement of position

An antique spectroscope

Prism, or grating, splits light into a spectrum

Annie Jump Cannon

Astronomer Annie Jump Cannon pioneered the classification of stars. Her work led to the division of the stars into different spectral types.

The variety of stars

Studying the spectra of stars tells us all about their composition, color, temperature, speed of travel, and spin. Other techniques allow astronomers to measure the distance to stars and their mass. Stars vary enormously. There are dwarfs with only a hundredth the diameter of the Sun and supergiants hundreds of times the Sun's size.

Supergiants are the biggest stars of all, hundreds of millions of miles across

Colors and sizes
A range of typical stars is shown across this page. The most luminous are at the top, the hottest on the left, and the coolest on the right. Stars get bigger as luminosity increases, and the most luminous are either bright blue or orange-red. A star's color is governed by the amount of energy pumping out of its surface.

Blue stars are tens of times bigger than the Sun

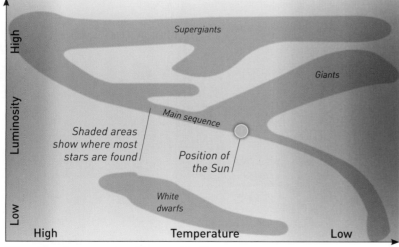

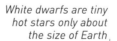

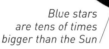

Supergiants

Giants

Main sequence

Shaded areas show where most stars are found

Position of the Sun

White dwarfs

High

Luminosity

Low

High   Temperature   Low

The Hertzsprung-Russell diagram
The Hertzsprung-Russell (HR) diagram looks at the relationships between the luminosity of stars, and their color and temperature. The majority of stars lie along a diagonal strip from faint red to bright blue.

White dwarfs are tiny hot stars only about the size of Earth

Line of main sequence

First dwarf
Stars similar to the Sun end their lives as white dwarfs, which gradually fade away. Sirius B (left, top) was the first white dwarf discovered.

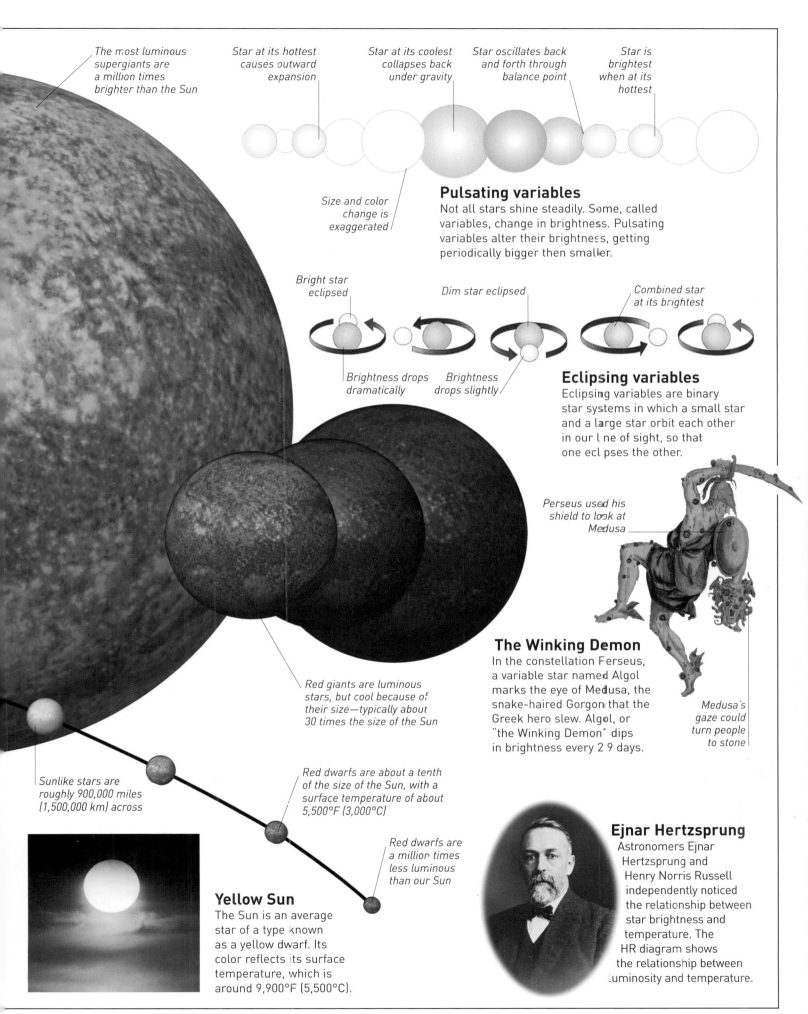

The most luminous supergiants are a million times brighter than the Sun

Star at its hottest causes outward expansion

Star at its coolest collapses back under gravity

Star oscillates back and forth through balance point

Star is brightest when at its hottest

Size and color change is exaggerated

Pulsating variables

Not all stars shine steadily. Some, called variables, change in brightness. Pulsating variables alter their brightness, getting periodically bigger then smaller.

Bright star eclipsed

Dim star eclipsed

Combined star at its brightest

Brightness drops dramatically

Brightness drops slightly

Eclipsing variables

Eclipsing variables are binary star systems in which a small star and a large star orbit each other in our line of sight, so that one eclipses the other.

Perseus used his shield to look at Medusa

Red giants are luminous stars, but cool because of their size—typically about 30 times the size of the Sun

The Winking Demon

In the constellation Perseus, a variable star named Algol marks the eye of Medusa, the snake-haired Gorgon that the Greek hero slew. Algol, or "the Winking Demon" dips in brightness every 2.9 days.

Medusa's gaze could turn people to stone

Sunlike stars are roughly 900,000 miles (1,500,000 km) across

Red dwarfs are about a tenth of the size of the Sun, with a surface temperature of about 5,500°F (3,000°C)

Red dwarfs are a million times less luminous than our Sun

Yellow Sun

The Sun is an average star of a type known as a yellow dwarf. Its color reflects its surface temperature, which is around 9,900°F (5,500°C).

Ejnar Hertzsprung

Astronomers Ejnar Hertzsprung and Henry Norris Russell independently noticed the relationship between star brightness and temperature. The HR diagram shows the relationship between luminosity and temperature.

Clusters and nebulae

In many parts of the heavens there are fuzzy patches. Some patches are groupings of stars, known as clusters. Open clusters are loose collections of a few hundred stars and globular clusters are dense groupings of thousands of stars. Other fuzzy patches are regions of glowing gas, called nebulae. They are the visible part of the interstellar medium.

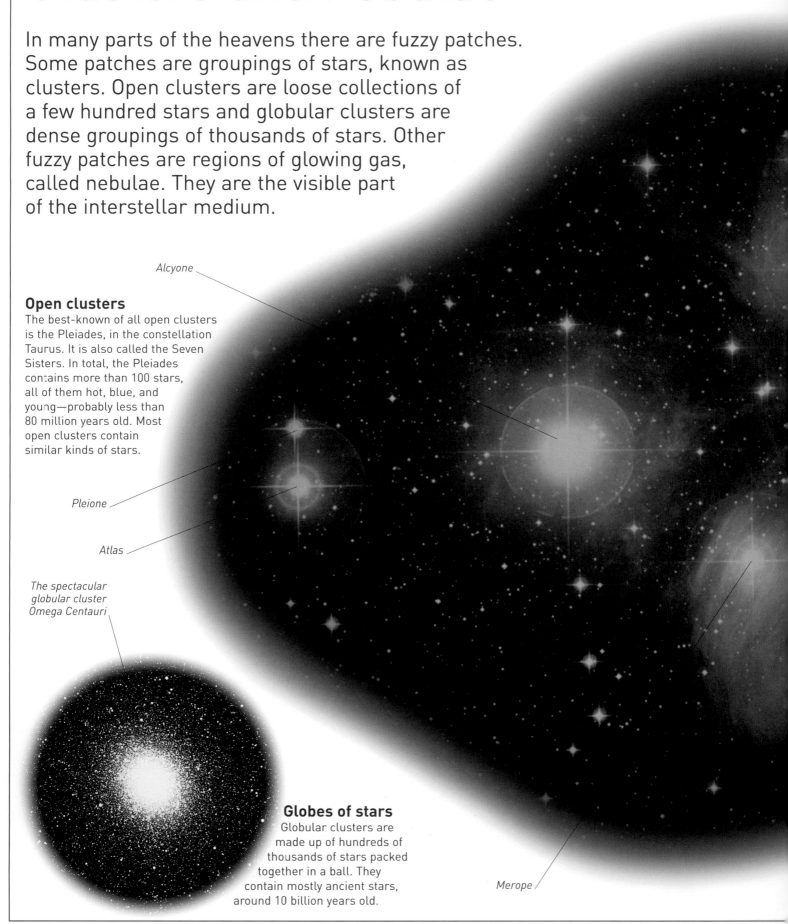

Alcyone

Open clusters
The best-known of all open clusters is the Pleiades, in the constellation Taurus. It is also called the Seven Sisters. In total, the Pleiades contains more than 100 stars, all of them hot, blue, and young—probably less than 80 million years old. Most open clusters contain similar kinds of stars.

Pleione

Atlas

The spectacular globular cluster Omega Centauri

Globes of stars
Globular clusters are made up of hundreds of thousands of stars packed together in a ball. They contain mostly ancient stars, around 10 billion years old.

Merope

Between the stars

The interstellar medium occupies the space between the stars and is made up mainly of hydrogen gas and specks of dust. The interstellar medium is visible as both bright and dark nebulae, and accounts for a tenth of the mass of our Galaxy.

Asterope

Taygeta

Maia

Celaeno

Electra

Reflection nebula

Dark nebulae
Some clouds of gas and dust are lit up, while others remain dark. The aptly named Horsehead Nebula (above) is a well-known dark nebula in Orion. Dark nebulae are generally cold, around -436°F (-260°C).

The Orion Nebula, M42

Bright nebulae
Many interstellar gas clouds are lit up by stars. Sometimes the clouds reflect starlight, and sometimes radiation embedded within the clouds cause their gas molecules to emit radiation. These emission nebulae include the Orion Nebula constellation (above).

M42's position in Orion

Stellar remnants
Stars are born from nebulae, and give rise to nebulae when they die. Stars like the Sun first swell up to become red giants, then shrink into tiny white dwarfs. As they do so, they puff off layers of gas, which become planetary nebulae.

Messier's comets
Astronomer Charles Messier was nicknamed the "ferret of comets" for discovering 15 new comets. He also compiled a catalog of 104 star clusters and nebulae.

Star birth

Stars are born in giant molecular clouds that occupy interstellar space. Within these clouds, made mainly of hydrogen, gravity pulls the gas molecules together to make denser clumps, and even denser cores. As gravity makes a core collapse in on itself, it becomes hotter and more compressed. When its temperature reaches 18 million°F (10 million°C), it becomes a new star.

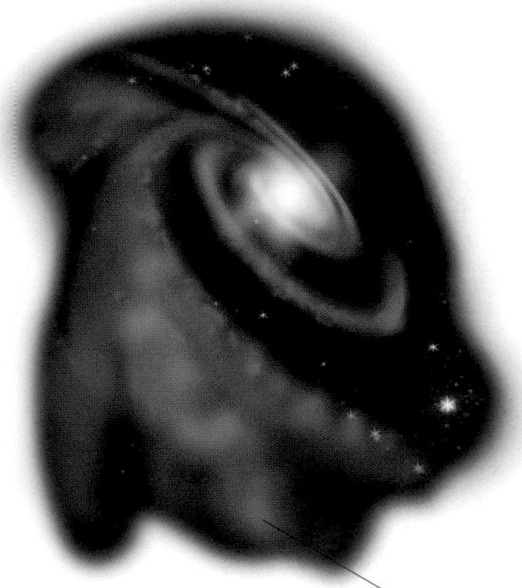

Matter spirals in

In a whirl

When cores of matter collapse during star formations, they start to rotate and heat up. The collapsing matter forms into a disk as a result of the rotation.

EGG

Collapsing gas clouds

Stellar nurseries

Stars are being born in vast numbers in giant molecular clouds everywhere, such as M16, the Eagle Nebula. Telescope pictures show dark columns nicknamed "the pillars of creation," where star formation takes place. Below, the top of one pillar shows fingerlike blobs of gas called evaporating gaseous globules (EGGs) where material is collapsing to form stars.

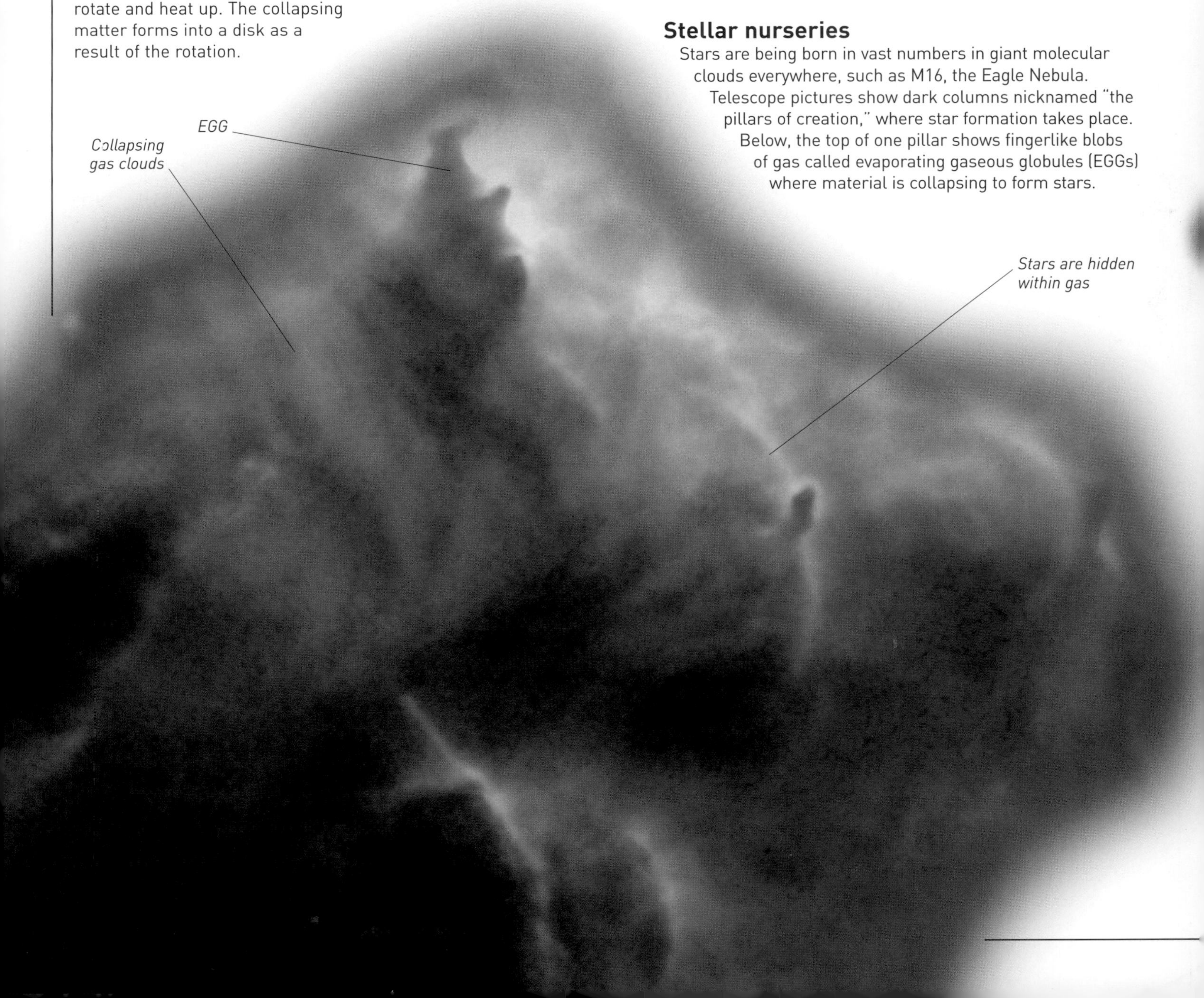

Stars are hidden within gas

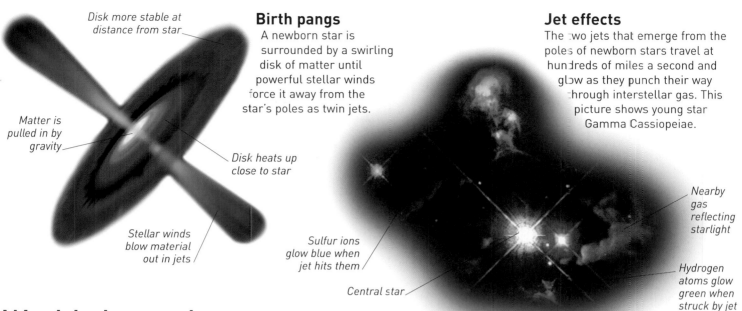

Birth pangs
A newborn star is surrounded by a swirling disk of matter until powerful stellar winds force it away from the star's poles as twin jets.

Disk more stable at distance from star

Matter is pulled in by gravity

Disk heats up close to star

Stellar winds blow material out in jets

Jet effects
The two jets that emerge from the poles of newborn stars travel at hundreds of miles a second and glow as they punch their way through interstellar gas. This picture shows young star Gamma Cassiopeiae.

Nearby gas reflecting starlight

Hydrogen atoms glow green when struck by jet

Sulfur ions glow blue when jet hits them

Central star

Worlds beyond

Newborn stars blow most of the matter surrounding them into space, but sometimes a disk of material remains. It is from such disks that planetary systems form.

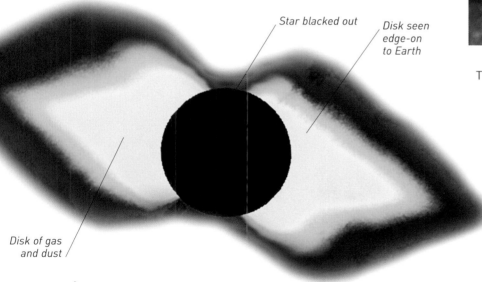

Star blacked out

Disk seen edge-on to Earth

Disk of gas and dust

The hidden millions
The Orion Nebula is a close star-forming region. In visible light (above left), glowing gas hides most of the nebula's young stars. But viewed in the infrared (above right), stars including red and brown dwarfs, become visible.

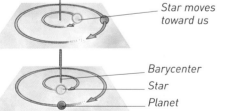

Star moves toward us

Barycenter
Star
Planet

Star moves away

Looking for planets
The planets around other stars are too faint to be seen. Astronomers find them by observing the effect they have on their star. As planet and star both orbit a shared center of gravity, we can detect their motion by examining the shift in the star's spectrum.

Planets in formation
Space telescopes such as IRAS (Infrared Astronomy Satellite) began detecting disks of material around other stars in the 1980s. One is Beta Pictoris, shown above.

Extrasolar planets
Astronomers detected the first extrasolar planets (planets that do not orbit around our Sun) in 1991, orbiting a dead star called a pulsar. Four years later, a planet was found around the Sun-like 51 Pegasi.

Star death

Stars burst into life by fusing hydrogen into helium in nuclear reactions in their cores. They shine until they use up their hydrogen fuel—then they start to die. First they brighten and swell into red giants and supergiants. Low-mass stars puff off their outer layers and fade away. High-mass stars die in a supernova explosion.

Fates of stars
How long a star can keep burning hydrogen depends on its mass. Stars like the Sun burn their fuel slowly and can shine for 10 billion years.

Live fast, die young
Stars bigger than the Sun have hotter, denser cores. They burn their hydrogen fuel more quickly and live for only a few million years.

Core develops "onion layers"

New fusion produces elements sodium, magnesium, silicon, and sulfur

Heaviest element produced is iron

Core (not shown to scale)

Red giant
When a star uses up the hydrogen in its core, fusion moves out to a shell around the center. The star's atmosphere then balloons outward. As the surface cools, the star becomes a red dwarf. As the core collapses, nuclear reactions give the star two million years of life.

Supergiant
In massive stars the core gets so hot that the star balloons out to become a supergiant, which is many times larger than a normal red giant.

Planetary nebula
When the helium in a red giant's core runs out, it blows the star's layers into space. Radiation then forms ring-shaped planetary nebula.

White dwarf

Within a planetary nebula, the star's core continues to collapse until the electrons in its atoms are forced up against the central nuclei. This incredibly dense, hot star is called a white dwarf.

Supernova

Iron builds up rapidly in a supergiant's core. When the core runs out of other fuel, it suddenly collapses. So much energy is released that the star blasts itself apart in a supernova explosion that can outshine a galaxy. The explosion scatters heavy elements across space, providing material for new stars.

Neutron star

Black hole

End states

Depending on the mass of the collapsing core, a supernova can either turn into a small, dense neutron star, or a black hole.

Supernova

In 1987, astronomers spotted a supernova (left) in the Large Magellanic Cloud, a close galaxy. The star that exploded was a blue giant called Sanduleak (far left).

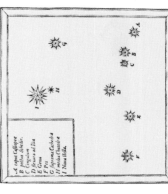

Supernovae in history

Tycho Brahe saw a supernova in 1572 (above, top), which caused him to realize that the heavens were not unchanging.

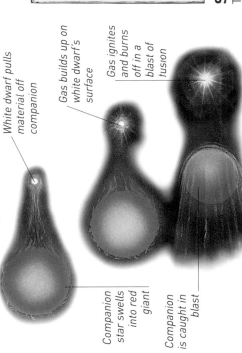

White dwarf pulls material off companion

Gas builds up on white dwarf's surface

Gas ignites and burns off in a blast of fusion

Companion star swells into red giant

Companion is caught in blast

Novae

A white dwarf in a binary system can attract enough gas from the other star to cause an explosion and make it into a nova, a new star.

Black holes

When a star dies in a supernova, the force of the collapsing core is so great that atoms are broken down. The matter then turns into packed neutrons and the core becomes a city-sized neutron star, spinning as it emits pulses of radiation. When we detect pulses from a neutron star, we call it a pulsar. Larger collapsing cores crush the neutrons and make a dense core that light cannot escape from—a black hole.

The crab pulsar
In 1054, Chinese astronomers saw a supernova explosion, which created the famous Crab Nebula. Buried inside the nebula is the collapsed core, which we detect as a pulsar.

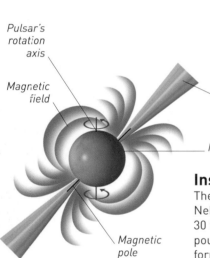

Pulsar's rotation axis

Magnetic field

Inner ring one light-year across

Jets from magnetic poles

Neutron star

Magnetic pole

Neutron stars
Neutron stars are tiny bodies that spin around rapidly. They are highly magnetic, so their magnetic field sweeps around rapidly as well. This generates radio waves, which are emitted as beams that we can see as pulsing signals.

Inside the crab
The pulsar in the Crab Nebula spins around 30 times a second and pours out energy in the form of radio waves and X-rays.

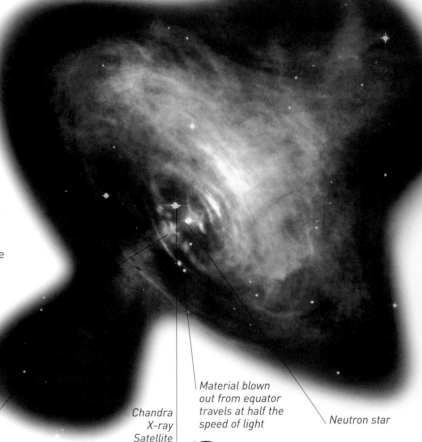

Jet from pulsar poles

Pulsar jet billows into clouds as it contacts interstellar gas

Chandra X-ray Satellite

Material blown out from equator travels at half the speed of light

Neutron star

Superdense matter
A neutron star is typically only 12 miles (20 km) across. Yet it contains the mass of up to three Suns, making it incredibly dense. Just a pinhead of neutron-star matter would weigh more than the world's heaviest supertanker.

Pulsar find
In 1967, astronomy student Jocelyn Bell picked up signals pulsating every 1.337 seconds. It was the first pulsar to be found, now called PSR 1919+21.

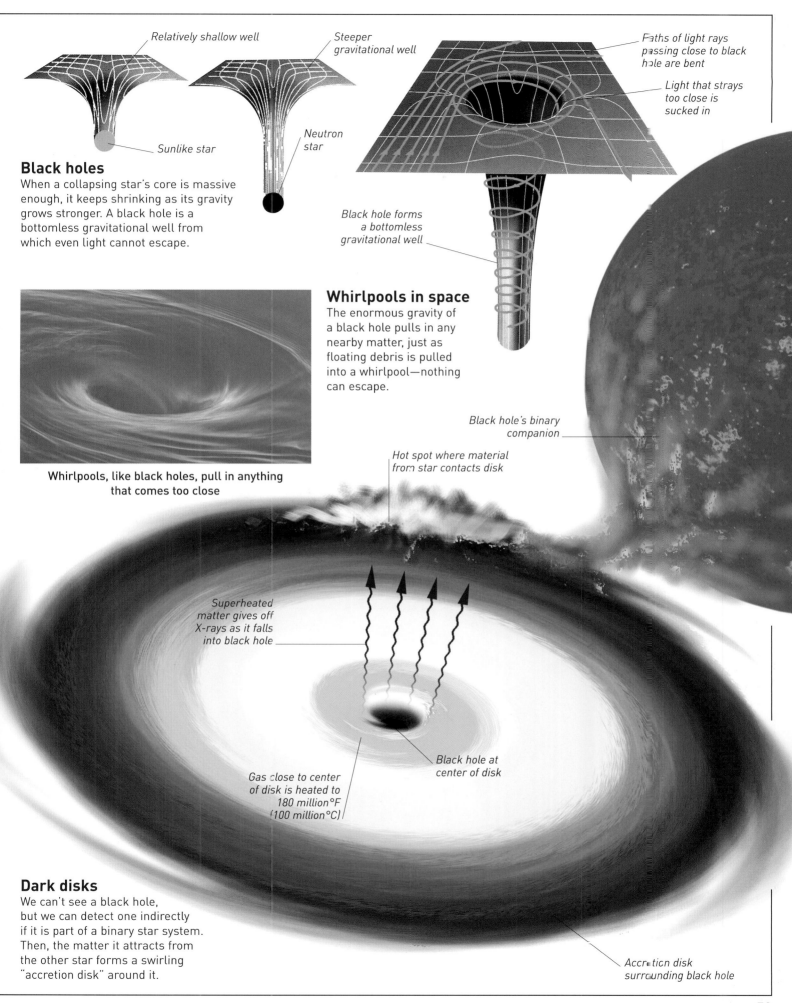

Black holes

When a collapsing star's core is massive enough, it keeps shrinking as its gravity grows stronger. A black hole is a bottomless gravitational well from which even light cannot escape.

Relatively shallow well

Sunlike star

Steeper gravitational well

Neutron star

Paths of light rays passing close to black hole are bent

Light that strays too close is sucked in

Black hole forms a bottomless gravitational well

Whirlpools in space

The enormous gravity of a black hole pulls in any nearby matter, just as floating debris is pulled into a whirlpool—nothing can escape.

Whirlpools, like black holes, pull in anything that comes too close

Black hole's binary companion

Hot spot where material from star contacts disk

Superheated matter gives off X-rays as it falls into black hole

Gas close to center of disk is heated to 180 million °F (100 million °C)

Black hole at center of disk

Dark disks

We can't see a black hole, but we can detect one indirectly if it is part of a binary star system. Then, the matter it attracts from the other star forms a swirling "accretion disk" around it.

Accretion disk surrounding black hole

The Milky Way

On a clear night, a hazy band of light arches across the heavens, running through many of the best-known constellations. We call it the Milky Way. What we are seeing is a kind of "slice" through the star system, or galaxy, to which the Sun and all the other stars in the sky belong. It passes through Cygnus, Perseus, and Cassiopeia in the northern hemisphere, and Centaurus, Crux, and Sagittarius in the southern hemisphere.

Milky Way myths
In the mythology of the Aztecs, the Milky Way was identified with Mixcoatl, the cloud-serpent god. In ancient Egypt and India, it was seen as the celestial mirror of rivers like the Nile and Ganges.

Star-forming molecular clouds

Anatomy of the galaxy
Our Galaxy is a vast system of around 500 billion stars. It measures 100,000 light-years across, but is mostly only about 2,000 light-years thick. The spiral arms around the central bulge form the disk of the galaxy. There are two major arms, the Scutum-Centaurus, and the Perseus, and several minor arms and spurs.

Scutum-Centaurus arm

Milky Way star clouds in Scorpius and Sagittarius

The backbone of night
The Milky Way's brightest areas are most visible between June and September. Its dark patches are not starless regions, but areas in which dense dust clouds block the light from the stars behind them.

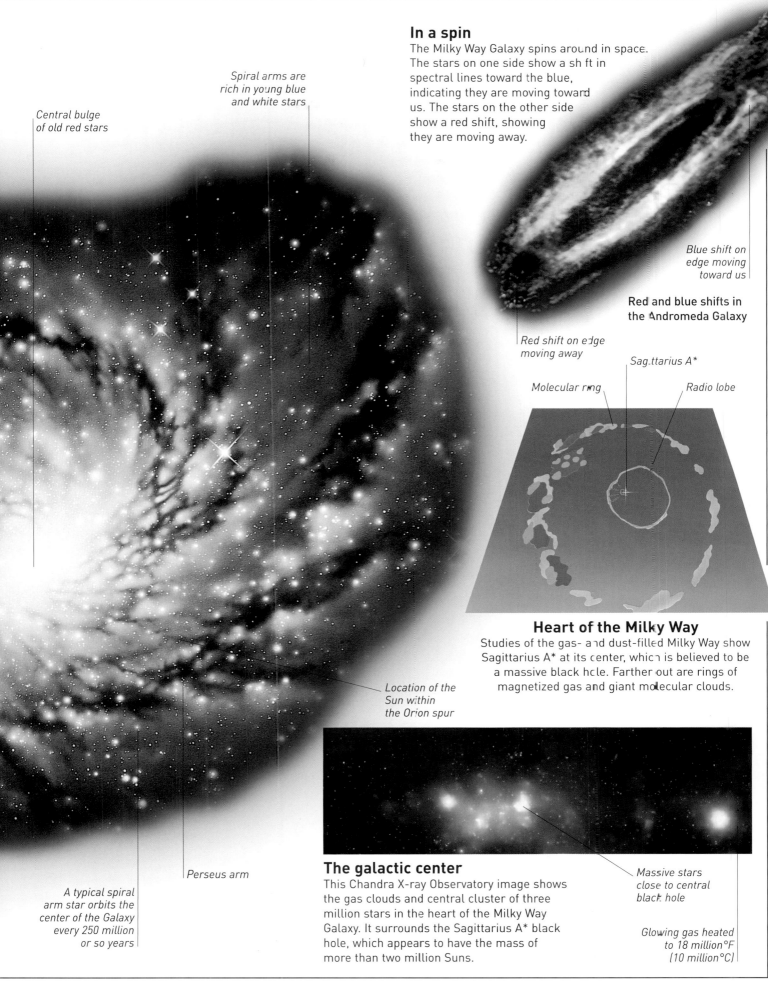

Central bulge
of old red stars

Spiral arms are
rich in young blue
and white stars

In a spin

The Milky Way Galaxy spins around in space. The stars on one side show a shift in spectral lines toward the blue, indicating they are moving toward us. The stars on the other side show a red shift, showing they are moving away.

Blue shift on
edge moving
toward us

Red and blue shifts in the Andromeda Galaxy

Red shift on edge
moving away

Sagittarius A*

Molecular ring

Radio lobe

Heart of the Milky Way

Studies of the gas- and dust-filled Milky Way show Sagittarius A* at its center, which is believed to be a massive black hole. Farther out are rings of magnetized gas and giant molecular clouds.

Location of the
Sun within
the Orion spur

Perseus arm

A typical spiral
arm star orbits the
center of the Galaxy
every 250 million
or so years

The galactic center

This Chandra X-ray Observatory image shows the gas clouds and central cluster of three million stars in the heart of the Milky Way Galaxy. It surrounds the Sagittarius A* black hole, which appears to have the mass of more than two million Suns.

Massive stars
close to central
black hole

Glowing gas heated
to 18 million°F
(10 million°C)

Neighbors

In far southern skies, two misty patches can be seen in the constellations Tucana and Dorado. They are nearby galaxies called the Large and Small Magellanic Clouds. The Large Magellanic Cloud lies just 160,000 light-years away and is irregular in shape, as is the Small Magellanic Cloud. The Magellanic Clouds and some smaller dwarf elliptical galaxies are not just neighbors of the Milky Way; they also come under its gravitational influence.

Magellan's clouds
The Magellanic Clouds are named after Portuguese navigator Ferdinand Magellan, who voyaged around the world in 1519.

Small Magellanic Cloud

Large Magellanic Cloud

Satellite galaxies
The Large Magellanic Cloud is 30,000 light-years across, less than one-third the size of the Milky Way. It contains much the same mix of stars and gas as our own galaxy. The Small Magellanic Cloud is only a quarter as big as the Large Cloud and lies slightly farther away.

The Local Group
The Milky Way is part of a larger collection of galaxies called the Local Group, which includes two more spiral galaxies in the constellations Andromeda and Triangulum. In all, there are more than 40 galaxies in the Local Group, which are bound loosely together by gravity.

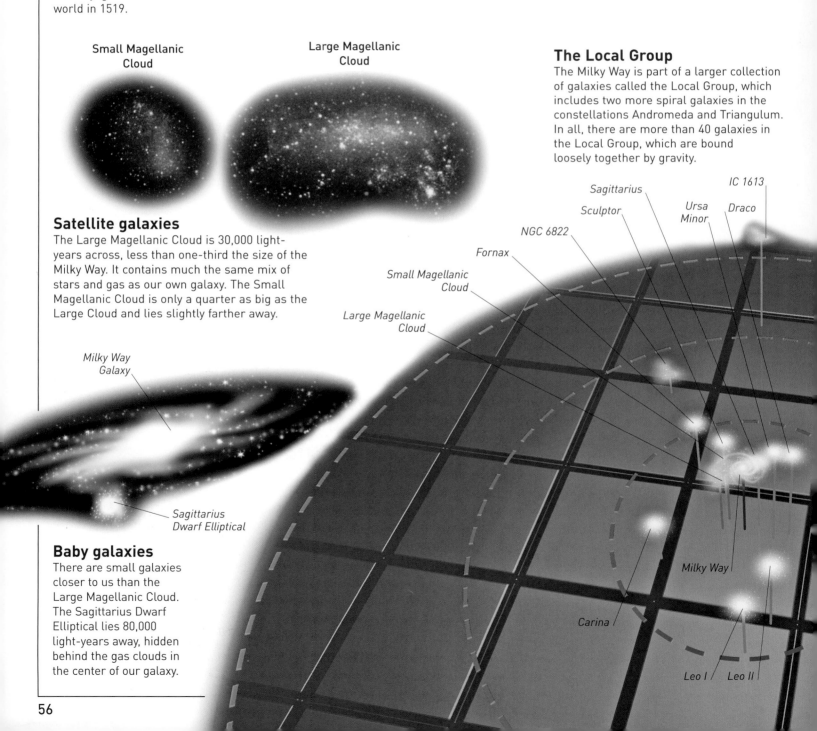

Milky Way Galaxy

Sagittarius Dwarf Elliptical

Sagittarius

Sculptor

Ursa Minor

IC 1613

Draco

NGC 6822

Fornax

Small Magellanic Cloud

Large Magellanic Cloud

Carina

Milky Way

Leo I

Leo II

Baby galaxies
There are small galaxies closer to us than the Large Magellanic Cloud. The Sagittarius Dwarf Elliptical lies 80,000 light-years away, hidden behind the gas clouds in the center of our galaxy.

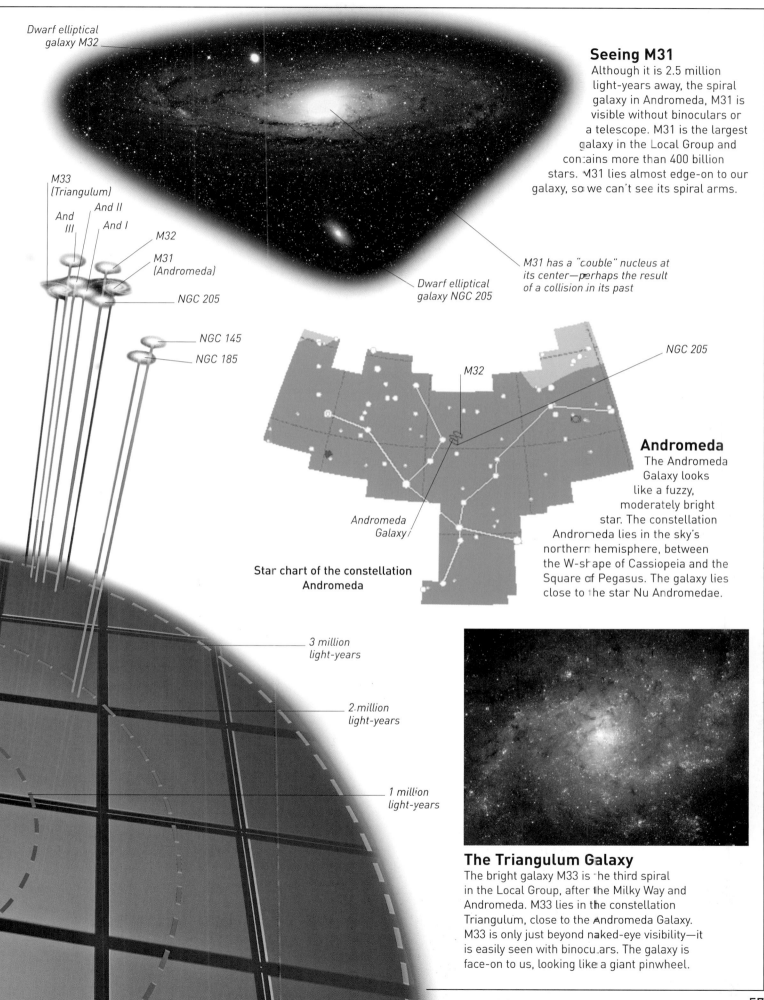

Dwarf elliptical galaxy M32

Seeing M31
Although it is 2.5 million light-years away, the spiral galaxy in Andromeda, M31 is visible without binoculars or a telescope. M31 is the largest galaxy in the Local Group and contains more than 400 billion stars. M31 lies almost edge-on to our galaxy, so we can't see its spiral arms.

M31 has a "double" nucleus at its center—perhaps the result of a collision in its past

M33 (Triangulum)

And III

And II

And I

M32

M31 (Andromeda)

NGC 205

NGC 145

NGC 185

Dwarf elliptical galaxy NGC 205

NGC 205

M32

Andromeda Galaxy

Star chart of the constellation Andromeda

Andromeda
The Andromeda Galaxy looks like a fuzzy, moderately bright star. The constellation Andromeda lies in the sky's northern hemisphere, between the W-shape of Cassiopeia and the Square of Pegasus. The galaxy lies close to the star Nu Andromedae.

3 million light-years

2 million light-years

1 million light-years

The Triangulum Galaxy
The bright galaxy M33 is the third spiral in the Local Group, after the Milky Way and Andromeda. M33 lies in the constellation Triangulum, close to the Andromeda Galaxy. M33 is only just beyond naked-eye visibility—it is easily seen with binoculars. The galaxy is face-on to us, looking like a giant pinwheel.

Galaxies galore

The Milky Way and the galaxies in the Local Group occupy only a tiny region of space. Scattered throughout the rest of space, across tens of billions of light-years, are at least 125 billion other galaxies. Many are spiral in shape, like the Milky Way. Others are oval, or elliptical, or have no regular shape at all. Some galaxies are dwarfs, with less than a million stars, but others are giants with hundreds of billions.

Colliding galaxies

Typically, adjacent galaxies are 10 galaxy diameters apart. From time to time, the vast gas clouds inside the galaxies crash into one another. This crashing together triggers bouts of furious star formation, known as starbursts.

Stars are flung out of both galaxies during collision

Elliptical galaxies classified E0–E9 in order of increasing ellipticity

Elliptical galaxies (E)

Spiral galaxy NGC 2207

Barred spiral galaxies (SB)

Spiral galaxies (S)

Spirals and barred spirals classified Sa–Sc and SBa–SBc, depending on the structure of their arms

Colliding galaxies NGC 2207 and IC 2163

Galaxy shapes

Edwin Hubble devised the method to classify galaxies as ellipticals (E), spirals (S), and barred spirals (SB), according to their shape.

Starburst region—a vast stellar nursery

Irregular galaxies

Galaxies with no particular shape are classed as irregulars, such as M82 in Ursa Major (left). Irregular galaxies are rich in gas and dust and have many young stars.

Clusters and superclusters

All galaxies interact with one another. Gravity binds them together into small groups and big clusters, which make up larger superclusters. Strings of superclusters form the structure of the universe.

Galaxy cluster Abell 2218

Stars orbit at many different angles

Elliptical galaxies contain old yellow stars

Elliptical galaxies

Elliptical galaxies include the smallest and largest galaxies. The biggest are a million light-years across. Giant ellipticals like M87 (right) are found in the heart of galaxy clusters.

Collision triggers bursts of star formation

Jet emerging from galaxy core

Spiral galaxy IC 2163

Silhouetted dust lane in NGC 2207

Larger galaxy's gravity distorts smaller galaxy

Lenticular galaxies

Lens-shaped lenticular galaxies are a cross between spiral and elliptical galaxies. They are spirals without the spiral arms and contain a central bulge of old stars.

Lenticular galaxy NGC 2787

How far?

Edwin Hubble (left) was the first to measure the distance to galaxies by using Cepheid variables. This means measuring a Cepheid star's true brightness against its apparent brightness to calculate its distance from Earth.

Active galaxies

Most galaxies give out the energy of hundreds of billions of stars shining together, but active galaxies give out much more. Active galaxies include radio galaxies, blazars, Seyfert galaxies, and the intriguing quasars. Their name is short for "quasi-stellar radio source," because they look like faint stars and give off radio waves. Powerful telescopes reveal that they are, in fact, galaxies with very bright centers, billions of light-years away. Black holes may give quasars their energy.

Looking at quasars
In 1960, astronomer Allan Sandage helped discover quasars when he linked radio source 3C48 with a starlike object, later identified as a quasar with a large red shift.

Radio galaxies
NGC 5128 is an elliptical galaxy and the nearest active galaxy to us, at just 15 million light-years away. This picture combines optical X-ray (blue) and radio (red and green) views of the central region. A halo of gas surrounds the galaxy.

Camera

Polished metal mirror assembly used to reflect and focus X-rays

Solar panels

Active galaxies
Violent activity in active galaxies produces high-energy radiation such as X-rays and gamma rays, which is observed by the Chandra X-ray Observatory (above).

Faint spiral arms 36,000 light-years across

Ring of intense starbirth around core

Bright core powered by black hole

Seyfert galaxy NGC 7742

Seyfert galaxies
Some spiral galaxies have particularly bright centers and are classed as Seyfert galaxies. They are now thought to be closer and less powerful versions of quasars. About one in 10 large spiral galaxies appear to be Seyferts.

Distant quasars
The Hubble Space Telescope spotted this quasar (center left), emitting radiation as visible light. The quasar's powerful energy emission is fueled by a collision between two galaxies.

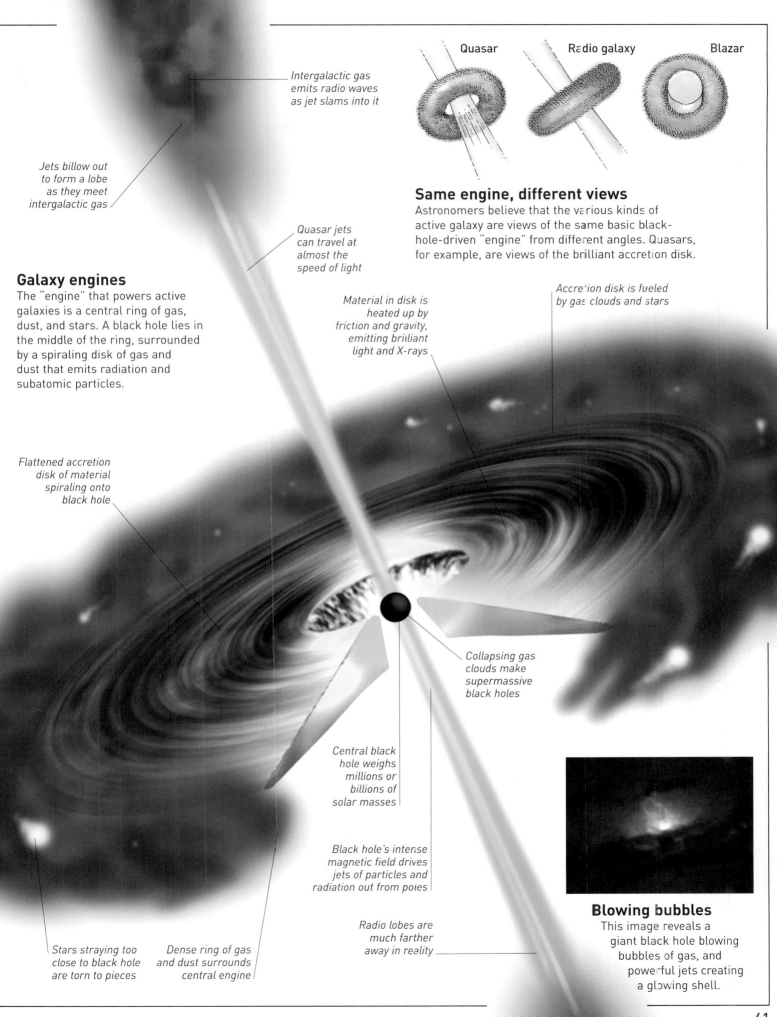

Intergalactic gas
emits radio waves
as jet slams into it

Jets billow out
to form a lobe
as they meet
intergalactic gas

Quasar jets
can travel at
almost the
speed of light

Quasar   Radio galaxy   Blazar

Same engine, different views

Astronomers believe that the various kinds of
active galaxy are views of the same basic black-
hole-driven "engine" from different angles. Quasars,
for example, are views of the brilliant accretion disk.

Galaxy engines

The "engine" that powers active
galaxies is a central ring of gas,
dust, and stars. A black hole lies in
the middle of the ring, surrounded
by a spiraling disk of gas and
dust that emits radiation and
subatomic particles.

Material in disk is
heated up by
friction and gravity,
emitting brilliant
light and X-rays

Accretion disk is fueled
by gas clouds and stars

Flattened accretion
disk of material
spiraling onto
black hole

Collapsing gas
clouds make
supermassive
black holes

Central black
hole weighs
millions or
billions of
solar masses

Black hole's intense
magnetic field drives
jets of particles and
radiation out from poles

Radio lobes are
much farther
away in reality

Stars straying too
close to black hole
are torn to pieces

Dense ring of gas
and dust surrounds
central engine

Blowing bubbles

This image reveals a
giant black hole blowing
bubbles of gas, and
powerful jets creating
a glowing shell.

A universe of life

We know of no other planet where life exists—but surely there is other life "out there." With billions of stars like the Sun in our galaxy alone, some of them must have planets capable of supporting life. Maybe intelligent life will find a way of communicating with us across space.

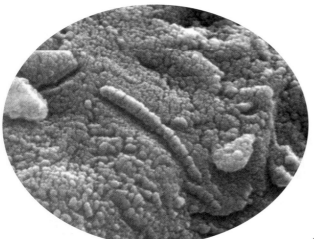
Crab on a volcanic vent

Extremes of life
Scientists now know life can thrive in hostile environments, like deep-sea crabs living by volcanic vents spewing out 660°F (350°C) sulfuric water.

Possible fossil bacteria in Martian meteorite

Life on Mars?
Mars is inhospitable to life now, but it probably had a more suitable climate long ago. If extraterrestrial life gained a foothold at that time, it could have left fossils to be discovered in the Martian soil.

Harbingers of life
Many carbon-based, organic molecules have been found in the gas clouds that exist between the stars. This suggests that life might be common in the universe.

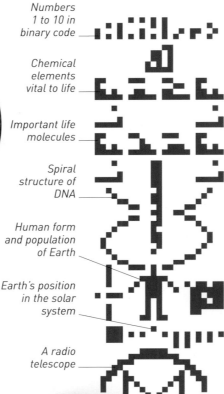

Numbers 1 to 10 in binary code

Chemical elements vital to life

Important life molecules

Spiral structure of DNA

Human form and population of Earth

Earth's position in the solar system

A radio telescope

Talking to aliens
The first message humankind transmitted to aliens was sent as a set of 1,679 on-off digital pulses. The message becomes clear when laid out in 73 rows of 23 columns. With black squares for 1s and white squares for 0s, a pattern or pictogram is produced that forms a message.

Arecibo calling
This message for alien life (left) was beamed at a cluster of 300,000 stars from the Arecibo radio telescope in 1974. It will reach them in 25,000 years.

Pictorial plaques
The Pioneer 10 and 11 and Voyager 1 and 2 space probes traveling out of the solar system are carrying messages for aliens on pictorial plaques and gold disks.

The chances of life

Frank Drake pioneered the use of radio telescopes to listen for signals from aliens. He also devised an equation (left) to estimate how many advanced civilizations are within our galaxy.

Energy trap

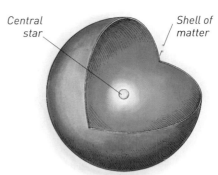

Central star

Shell of matter

Physicist Freeman Dyson has suggested that an advanced civilization may build a huge sphere around its star to trap energy.

What might they be like?

This low-browsing herbivore from Epsilon Reticulib is an imaginary alien invented by biologists. The alien has been designed to be well-suited to its environment in order to survive.

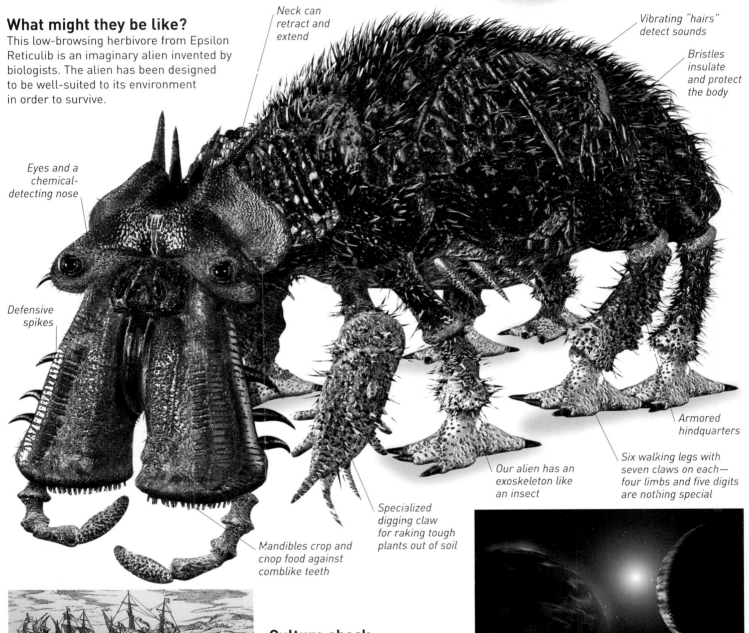

Neck can retract and extend

Vibrating "hairs" detect sounds

Bristles insulate and protect the body

Eyes and a chemical-detecting nose

Defensive spikes

Armored hindquarters

Six walking legs with seven claws on each— four limbs and five digits are nothing special

Our alien has an exoskeleton like an insect

Specialized digging claw for raking tough plants out of soil

Mandibles crop and chop food against comblike teeth

Culture shock

If contact with aliens occurs, the impact on humankind will be enormous. The clash in physical form and culture would be infinitely more shocking than when Columbus first met Native Americans in 1472 (left), and maybe as damaging.

Epsilon Reticuli

The hypothetical alien above comes from a moon of the planet Epsilon Reticuli b, 60 light-years from Earth. The planet orbits its star 20 percent farther out than Earth orbits the Sun.

Star maps

Earth's sky is divided into 88 constellations, or star patterns. These two maps will help you identify the constellations. The first shows stars visible from Earth's northern hemisphere, and the second from the southern hemisphere. Over the course of the year, as Earth orbits the Sun, different stars become visible.

Some stars within constellations are easy to spot, like the seven stars in the back of Ursa Major, the Great Bear. They are known as The Big Dipper.

The Big Dipper

Position of The Big Dipper in Ursa Major

Northern hemisphere stars

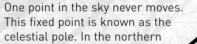

One point in the sky never moves. This fixed point is known as the celestial pole. In the northern hemisphere, North Star is almost exactly on the celestial north pole. It is the brightest star in the constellation of Ursa Minor.

Face south

Turn the book so the current month is at the bottom. Northern hemisphere observers should then face south to see the stars in the map's lower part.

This view of Taurus shows the star Aldebaran at upper left, above the Hyades star cluster.

The Double Cluster is two dense groupings of stars (left and right of center).

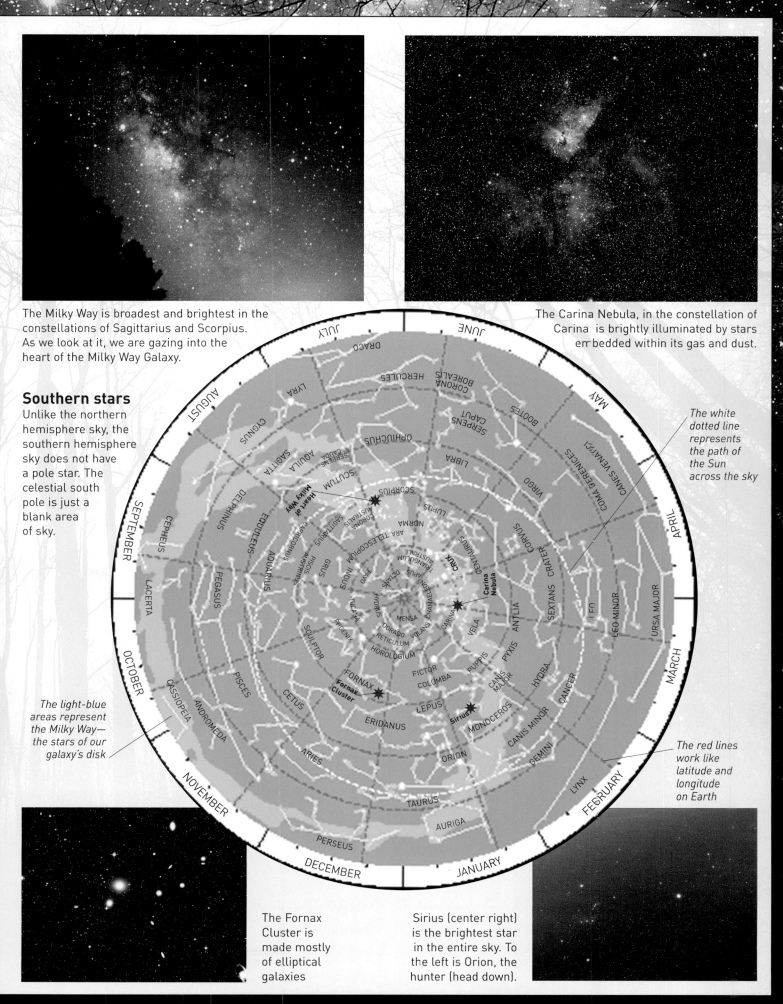

The Milky Way is broadest and brightest in the constellations of Sagittarius and Scorpius. As we look at it, we are gazing into the heart of the Milky Way Galaxy.

Southern stars

Unlike the northern hemisphere sky, the southern hemisphere sky does not have a pole star. The celestial south pole is just a blank area of sky.

The Carina Nebula, in the constellation of Carina is brightly illuminated by stars embedded within its gas and dust.

The white dotted line represents the path of the Sun across the sky

The light-blue areas represent the Milky Way— the stars of our galaxy's disk

The red lines work like latitude and longitude on Earth

The Fornax Cluster is made mostly of elliptical galaxies

Sirius (center right) is the brightest star in the entire sky. To the left is Orion, the hunter (head down).

Discovery timeline

Humans have studied the universe for at least 5,000 years. Recently, we have pieced together the universe's story, from its beginning in the Big Bang around 13.8 billion years ago, to the present day.

Saturn's rings, described correctly in 1655

The Crab Nebula, the remnant of a supernova seen in 1054

c. 4000 BCE The Egyptians, Chaldeans, and Hindus name bright stars and form them into constellations.

c. 2000 BCE Lunar and solar calendars are introduced.

550 BCE Pythagoras, a Greek mathematician, suggests that the Sun, Moon, Earth, and planets are spherical.

360 BCE The Greek philosopher Aristotle proposes that the planets are stuck in rotating crystal spheres, and that all stars are the same distance away. He states that the universe is made from a combination of fire, water, earth, and air.

290 BCE In Greece, the astronomer Aristarchus uses lunar eclipse timings to show that the distance between Earth and the Moon is equal to about 31 times Earth's width, and that the Moon is just over one-quarter the size of Earth.

150 BCE Hipparchus measures the length of the year to an accuracy of six minutes. He catalogs the position and brightness of stars, and states that the Sun's orbit around Earth is elliptical.

c. 130 CE Ptolemy writes *The Almagest*, which summarizes the astronomical knowledge of the time.

c. 800 Arab astronomers refine astronomical knowledge, including defining the ecliptic and the orbital periods of the Sun, Moon, and planets.

1054 Chinese astronomers record a supernova in the constellation of Taurus.

1252 In Spain, King Alphonso X commissions the Alphonsine Tables, which list planetary positions.

1420 The Mongol ruler Ulugh Beg builds an observatory in Samarkand. His catalog of naked-eye star positions is the first since that of Hipparchus.

1543 Nicolaus Copernicus, a Polish astronomer, publishes *On the Revolution of the Heavenly Spheres*. It signals the end of the idea of an Earth-centered universe.

1572 Danish nobleman Tycho Brahe observes a supernova in Cassiopeia, and shows that it lies beyond the Moon. Stars are thus not a fixed distance away.

1596 Tycho Brahe finishes 20 years of highly accurate planetary observations.

1609 German astronomer Johannes Kepler devises two laws. First, that planets have elliptical orbits, with the Sun at one focus of the ellipse. Second, that a planet moves fastest when close to the Sun.

1610 In Italy, Galileo Galilei publishes the results of his telescopic studies in *Siderius Nuncius*. These show that the Moon is mountainous, Jupiter has four Moons, and the Sun is spotted and rotates. Galileo states that the phases of Venus indicate that the Sun, not Earth, lies at the solar system's center.

1619 Johannes Kepler devises his third law, which describes the mathematical relationship between a planet's orbital period and its distance from the Sun.

1655 Christiaan Huygens, a Dutch mathematician and astronomer, correctly describes Saturn's ring system and discovers Saturn's moon, Titan.

1675 In Denmark, Ole Römer uses the eclipse times of Jupiter's moons to measure the speed of light.

1686 English astronomer Edmond Halley shows that "his" comet is periodic and part of the solar system. It sweeps past the Sun every 76 years.

1687 Isaac Newton, an English physicist, publishes his theory of gravity in *Principia*. It explains why the planets orbit the Sun.

1761 and 1769 Astronomers observe the transits of Venus across the face of the Sun, which are used to calculate the distance between the Sun and Earth.

1769 The first predicted return of a comet (Halley's) proves that the laws of gravity extend at least to the edge of the solar system.

Willaim Herschel discovered Uranus in 1781

1781 William Herschel discovers the planet Uranus.

1784 A list of 103 "fuzzy" nebulae is drawn up by Frenchman Charles Messier.

1785 William Herschel describes the shape of the Milky Way Galaxy.

1801 Giuseppe Piazzi, an Italian monk, discovers Ceres, the first asteroid.

1815 Joseph von Fraunhofer maps the dark lines in the solar spectrum.

1838 German astronomer Friedrich Bessel calculates that the star 61 Cygni is 11 light-years away.

1840 In the US, the Moon is photographed by John W. Draper. It is the first photo to record astronomical data.

1846 Neptune is discovered by using Newton's laws of gravitation.

1864 In England, William Huggins uses a spectrometer to show that comets contain carbon and that stars consist of the same chemical elements as Earth.

1890 About 30 stellar distances have now been measured.

1900 New knowledge of the radioactive decay of elements leads to the realization that the Earth is more than 1 billion years old.

1905 Albert Einstein proposes that E = mc², meaning that energy (E) can be produced by destroying mass (m). This is the breakthrough in understanding energy generation in stars.

1910 By plotting stellar temperature and luminosity, Ejnar Hertzsprung and Henry Russell find that there are only two main groups of stars: "dwarfs" and "giants."

1912 American Henrietta Leavitt finds that the time periods between the maximum brightnesses of Cepheid giant stars are related to their luminosities.

1917 The 100-inch (2.5-meter) Hooker Telescope on Mount Wilson, California, is used for the first time.

1920 American Harlow Shapley finds that the Sun is two-thirds of the way toward the edge of the Milky Way.

Charged-coupled device (CCD), 1980

1925 Cecilia Payne-Gaposchkin, an Anglo-American astronomer, shows that 75 percent of a star's mass is hydrogen.

1926 Arthur Eddington finds that for most of a star's life its luminosity is dependent on its mass.

Cecilia Payne-Gaposchkin, 1925

1927 American Edwin Hubble shows that the universe is expanding.

1930 Pluto is discovered by Clyde Tombaugh.

1931 Karl Jansky detects radio waves from the Milky Way's center.

1931 Georges Lemaître suggests that all matter in the universe started as a single, highly condensed sphere. This exploded in a "Big Bang."

1939 Physicist Hans Bethe shows how destroying hydrogen and producing helium yields stellar energy.

1955 Fred Hoyle and Martin Schwarzschild, show how helium changes into carbon and oxygen in giant stars, and how higher elements like cobalt and iron are made when massive stars explode.

1963 The first quasar, 3C48, is identified.

1965 Arno Penzias and Robert Wilson discover cosmic microwave background radiation.

1967 Belfast-born Jocelyn Bell-Burnell discovers the first pulsar.

1971 The first black hole Cygnus X-1 is discovered due to its effect on its companion star.

1980 In the US, Vera Rubin finds that many galaxies contain dark matter that affects their spin speed.

1980 US cosmologist Alan Guth modifies the Big Bang theory. He introduces "inflation," whereby the very young universe expands from the size of a proton to the size of a watermelon in an instant.

1980 Charged-coupled devices (the electronic chips in digital cameras) are used in astronomy. They are nearly 100 percent efficient at converting light into electronic signals.

1992 The first Kuiper Belt object is discovered by David Jewitt and Jane Luu.

1992 The first discovery of exoplanets—planets orbiting stars other than the Sun.

1995 The first exoplanet orbiting an ordinary main sequence star, 51 Pegasi, is discovered.

2006 The category of dwarf planets is introduced after the discovery of Eris. Pluto is reclassified as a dwarf planet.

2011 The Nobel Prize in Physics is awarded for the discovery of the accelerating expansion of the universe.

Dwarf planet Eris, 2006

Find out more

Books are a great way to find out about the universe, but you may want to be more than an armchair astronomer. Start by looking up and exploring the sky for yourself, or join a society of other amateur astronomers. You can also visit observatories, museums, and space centers.

Tanegashima Space Center, Japan

Space centers
Some space centers have public viewing areas where you can watch the launch of a rocket, or see space engineers preparing the next generation of spacecraft.

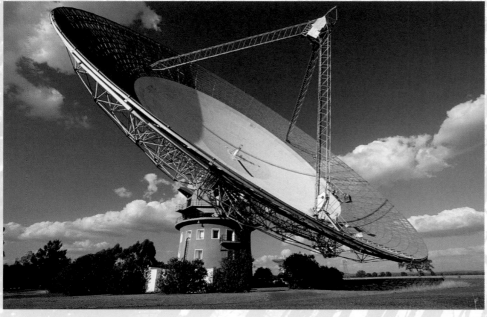

Parkes Radio Telescope, Australia

Radio telescopes
Unlike optical telescopes, radio telescopes are sited on low-lying ground and are more accessible. You can get up close to the telescopes, and learn about them in the visitor centers.

PLACES TO VISIT

KENNEDY SPACE CENTER, FLORIDA

This space complex sent men to the Moon and launched the Space Shuttles. Tour the exhibits and watch preparations for a future launch.

MAUNA KEA OBSERVATORIES, HAWAII

The domant volcano is home to 13 telescopes, including the Kecks, two of the largest telescopes in the world.

NOORDWIJK SPACE EXPO, NETHERLANDS

The European Space Agency's visitor exhibition tells the story of space exploration and has a planetarium showing simulations of space.

Observatories
Today's world-class optical observatories are built on mountaintop locations far from inhabited areas. Those situated at lower altitudes have public access programs. You can look around the observatory site and a few observatories will even let you gaze through a telescope.

Yerkes Observatory, US

Mexico City's planetarium

Planetariums and museums

A visit to a planetarium—an indoor theater where images of space are projected above your head—will help you become familiar with the night sky. Get to know the constellations before being transported across space to see planets and stars in close-up.

Tube houses mirror that collects and focuses starlight

Light enters telescope

Finder telescope to locate object

Eyepiece

Portable telescope for home and countryside

Mount supports telescope and automatically turns it to keep pace with the sky

Tripod stand

Viewing with binoculars

Home skywatching

On a clear, Moonless night in the city you will be able to pick out around 300 stars using your eyes alone, and 10 times more will be visible from a dark rural location. Binoculars reveal still more stars. Telescopes bring the objects even closer, making them appear brighter and larger.

Joining a group or society

Skywatching with others is a great way to learn. National societies and associations publish journals and hold meetings. You can also find local amateur astronomical organizations in many towns and cities. Some of these have their own telescopes and hold regular observing sessions.

Glossary

ACTIVE GALAXY A galaxy emitting an exceptional amount of energy, much of which comes from a central supermassive black hole.

ASTEROID A small rocky body orbiting the Sun. Most asteroids orbit in the Asteroid Belt between Mars and Jupiter.

ASTRONOMY The study of everything in space, including space itself.

ATMOSPHERE The layer of gas around a planet or moon, held in place by gravity.

AURORA The colorful light display of glowing gas in the upper atmosphere above a planet's polar regions.

BARRED SPIRAL GALAXY A galaxy with spiral arms that curl out from the ends of a bar-shaped nucleus.

BIG BANG The explosion that created the universe.

BINARY STAR A pair of stars, each of which revolves around the overall center of mass of the two-star system.

BLACK HOLE A compact region of space where mass has collapsed and whose gravity stops anything from escaping.

BRIGHTNESS A measure of the light of a star as seen from Earth (*see* Luminosity).

BROWN DWARF A star with too little mass to start the nuclear fusion process that powers a normal star.

CEPHEID A type of variable star whose brightness changes over time as the star alternately expands and contracts.

CLUSTER A group of stars or galaxies that are gravitationally bound together.

COMET A small body of snow, ice, and dust known as a nucleus that orbits the Sun beyond the planets.

Comet McNaught, 2007

Barringer Crater, Arizona

CONSTELLATION One of the 88 areas of the Earth's sky whose bright stars form an imaginary pattern.

CORONA The outermost region of the Sun's atmosphere.

COSMOLOGY The study of the universe as a whole, and its origin and evolution.

CRATER A bowl-shaped hollow in the surface of a planet or moon.

DARK ENERGY A form of energy that makes up 68 percent of the universe.

DARK MATTER Matter that makes up 27 percent of the universe.

DOUBLE STAR Two stars that appear very close together in Earth's sky, but which are in reality physically separate.

DWARF PLANET A near-spherical body orbiting the Sun.

ECLIPSE An effect due to the passage of one space body into the shadow of another. In a solar eclipse, the Moon covers the Sun. In a lunar eclipse, the Moon moves into Earth's shadow.

ECLIPTIC The yearly path followed by the Sun in Earth's sky.

ELECTROMAGNETIC RADIATION The energy waves given off by space objects. These include light, X-rays, and radio and infrared wavelengths.

ELLIPTICAL GALAXY A round- or elliptical-shaped galaxy.

EXTRASOLAR PLANET (EXOPLANET) A planet orbiting a star other than the Sun.

EXTRATERRESTRIAL LIFE A life-form not originating on Earth.

GALAXY A grouping of a vast number of stars, gas, and dust held together by gravity. The Sun is one of the stars in the Milky Way Galaxy.

GAS GIANT A large planet that consists predominantly of hydrogen and helium, which are in gaseous form at the planet's visible surface.

GLOBULAR CLUSTER A near-spherical cluster of old stars found predominantly in the halo of a galaxy.

GRAVITY A force of attraction found throughout the universe.

HERTZSPRUNG-RUSSELL (H-R) DIAGRAM A diagram in which stars are plotted according to their luminosity and surface temperature, and which shows different classes of stars, such as giants and dwarfs.

Neptune, a gas giant

INTERSTELLAR MEDIUM Gas and dust between the stars in a galaxy.

IRREGULAR GALAXY A galaxy with no obvious shape or structure.

KUIPER BELT The belt of rock and ice bodies that orbit the Sun beyond Neptune.

LENTICULAR GALAXY A galaxy in the shape of a convex lens.

LIGHT-YEAR A unit of distance. One light-year is the distance light travels in one year: 5.9 trillion miles (9.5 trillion km).

LOCAL GROUP The cluster of more than 40 galaxies that includes the Milky Way.

LUMINOSITY The total amount of energy emitted in one second by a star.

MAIN SEQUENCE STAR A star that shines steadily by converting hydrogen into helium.

MASS The amount of matter in an object.

METEOR A short-lived streak of light that is produced by a meteoroid as it travels through Earth's atmosphere.

METEORITE A piece of asteroid that has traveled through space and lands on a planet or moon.

MILKY WAY The barred, spiral-shaped galaxy that includes the Sun. Also the name of the path of stars in Earth's night sky that is our view of the galaxy's disk of stars.

MOON A body orbiting a planet or asteroid. Also called a natural satellite.

NEBULA A vast cloud of gas and dust in interstellar space (*see* Planetary nebula).

NEUTRON STAR An ultra-dense, compact star formed from the core of a star that explodes as a supernova.

NOVA A star that suddenly brightens at least a thousand-fold, and then fades back to normal brightness.

NUCLEAR FUSION The process that takes place within a star's core, whereby atomic nuclei join to form heavier atomic nuclei and energy is released.

NUCLEUS The body of a comet, the core of a galaxy, or the core of an atom.

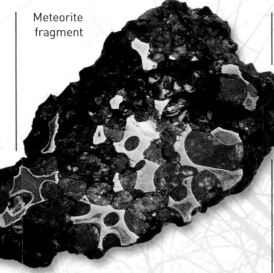

Meteorite fragment

OBSERVATORY A building or complex housing telescopes.

OORT CLOUD A sphere of more than a trillion comets surrounding the planetary part of the solar system.

ORBIT The path taken by a body around another of greater mass.

PHOTOSPHERE The gaseous but visible outer surface of the Sun, or other star.

PLANET A massive round body that orbits a star.

PLANETARY NEBULA A late stage in the life of a star such as the Sun.

PROTOSTAR An early stage in the formation of a star.

PULSAR A rapidly rotating neutron star identified by the brief pulses of energy we receive as it spins.

QUASAR An active galaxy that is compact and extremely luminous.

RADIO GALAXY An active galaxy that is exceptionally luminous.

RED GIANT A large, red, luminous star in its late stages.

SATELLITE A natural body orbiting another more massive body.

SEYFERT GALAXY An active spiral galaxy with a luminous and compact nucleus.

Cat's Eye Nebula (NGC 6543), a planetary nebula

SHOOTING STAR An everyday name for a meteor.

SOLAR CYCLE An 11-year period of varying solar activity.

SOLAR SYSTEM The Sun and all the bodies that orbit it.

SPACE The region beyond Earth's atmosphere in which all bodies exist.

SPECTRAL CLASS A star's classification according to the lines in its spectrum.

SPEED OF LIGHT The constant speed at which light travels: 186,000 miles per second (299,792,458 km per second).

SPIRAL GALAXY A disk-shaped galaxy with spiral arms.

STAR A huge spinning sphere of very hot and very luminous gas.

SUNSPOT A dark, cool region on the visible surface of the Sun or another star.

Spiral galaxy NGC 4414

SUPERCLUSTER A group of galaxy clusters.

SUPERGIANT A large, luminous star.

SUPERNOVA A massive star that has exploded and is up to a million times brighter than usual.

TELESCOPE An instrument that uses lenses or mirrors to collect and focus light to form an image of a distant object.

TERRESTRIAL PLANETS The solar system's four rocky planets: Mercury, Venus, Earth, and Mars.

UNIVERSE Everything that exists: all the galaxies, stars, and planets, and the space in between.

VARIABLE STAR A star whose brightness varies over time.

WHITE DWARF An end-stage in the life of a star.

Index

Acknowledgments

Dorling Kindersley would like to thank:
Darren Naish and Mark Longworth for
Epsilon Reticuli b Alien; Peter Bull for other
artworks; Jonathan Brooks and Sarah Mills
for picture research.

For this relaunch edition, the publisher
would also like to thank: Carole Stott for
assisting with the updates, Ben Hubbard
for editorial assistance, and Carron Brown
for proofreading.

Picture credits:
The publisher would like to thank the
following for their kind permission to
reproduce their photographs:

(Key: a-above; b-below/bottom; c-center;
f-far; l-left; r-right; t-top)
Agence France Presse: 52bl.akg-images:
39tr, 45br; Cameraphoto 40tl. **Alamy Images:**
Classic Image 66b; Danita Delimont / Russell
Gordon 59tc. **Anglo- Australian Observatory:**
David Malin 51tr. **The Art Archive:** Musée du
Louvre Paris / Dagli Orti (A) 27cr. **Bridgeman
Art Library, London / New York:** Archives
Charmet 47br. **British Museum:** 6bl. © **CERN
Geneva:** 2tr, 10bl. **Corbis:** 62bc; Lucien
Aigner 14tl; Yann Arthus-Bertrand 8cl;
Bettmann 3tl, 7tr, 12bl, 18tl, 32cl, 59br, 67cl;
Araldo de Luca 20tl; Dennis di Cicco 40–41cr;

Paul Hardy 14clb; Charles & Josette Lenars
70tc; NASA 8clb, 39br; Michael Neveux 4cr,
6c; Robert Y. Ono 45bl; Enzo & Paolo
Ragazzini 6bc; Roger Ressmeyer 4cl, 13tl,
17tr, 62cr, 68br, 68cl, 69bl; Paul A. Souders
29cr; Stapleton Collection 45cr; Brenda
Tharp 53cla; Robert Yin 29br. **DK Images:**
Natural History Museum, 71tc. **European
Space Agency:** 11crb; D. Ducros 17bl; ESA/
Hubble: NASA, S. Finkelstein (University of
Texas, Austin), C. Papovich and V. Tilvi (Texas
A&M University), and the CANDELS team
17bc; NASA 40c. **ESO:** Igor Chekalin 47c. ©
Stéphane Guisard: 70bl. **Courtesy of JAXA:**
68tr. **Mary Evans Picture Library:** 8tl, 26bc,
27crb, 31c, 41cr, 56tl, 63bl; Alvin Correa
31br. **Galaxy Picture Library:** 25tl, 56cl, 57c,
57br, 59cra. **Getty Images:** Barros & Barros
12tl; Sean Hunter: 29cra. **Kobal Collection:**
Universal 22c. **FLPA - Images of nature:** B.
Borrell 22cb, 22crb. **Fotolia:** Dundanim
6–7bc **NASA:** 2b, 2cl, 3tr, 5tr, 9c, 9bl (x6),
11tl, 16br, 17br, 18cl, 18c, 19tr, 23tr, 23ca,
23cr, 23br, 26, 27tr, 27br, 27br, 27l, 29cr, 30br,
31cr, 31ac, 33tr, 33bl, 35cra, 35bl, 35bc, 35ac,
37cr, 38–39c, 50–51b, 55br; CXC/JPL-Caltech
/STScI/NSF/NRAO/VLA 3c; JPL-Caltech
11crb; CXC/JPL-Caltech/STScI NSF/NRAO/
VLA 11br; JPL-Caltech/Space Science
Institute 18ca; Damian Peach 24cr; Johns
Hopkins University Applied Physics

Laboratory/Carnegie Institution of
Washington 26c; JPL-Caltech/Univ. of
Arizona 31cr; Craig Attebery 35br; AURA/
STScI 49cr; Boomerang Project 13c;
Carnegie Mellon University 39cr; W.N. Colley
and E. Turner (Princeton University), J.A.
Tyson (Bell Labs, Lucent Technologies) 15cr;
CXC/ASU/J 52c; X-ray: CXC, J.Hester (ASU)
et al. 52tr; ESA and The Hubble Heritage
Team (STScI/AURA) 47bc; HST Comet
Science Team 32bc; Institute of Space and
Astronautical Sciences, Japan 21tr; JHUAPL
39tl, 39tc; JPL 8ca, 32c, 32bl, 33tc, 33cra,
33c, 33ac, 36clb, 36bc, 18bl, 66cla, 66tr, 70cr;
JPL/University of Arizona 32-33; JPL/Space
Science Institute 66tr; JSC 62cl; NASA
HQ-GRIN 71cr; NOAO, ESA and The Hubble
Heritage Team (STScI/AURA) 47tr; SOHO
20bl; Courtesy of SOHO/Extreme Ultraviolet
Imaging Telescope (EIT) consortium 21bl;
STScI 7bc, 9tr, 43tl, 48b, 49cr, 49br, 58–59c,
59tc, 59bl, 60cl, 60bl, 60br, 61br; STScI/COBE
/ DIRBE Science Team 8bl; TRW 60cr; Dr. Hal
Weaver and T. Ed Smith (STScI) 40bl. **Musée
de la Poste, Paris:** 37c. **National Maritime
Museum:** 4tr, 7cra, 43bc; NOAA: OAR/
National Undersea Research Program
(NURP) 62tl. **NOAO/AURA/NSF:** N.A.Sharp
58; Pikaia: 2cra, 2crb, 4tl, 6-7, 9cl, 12bc,
14bl, 14-15, 15br, 24-25, 26tr, 27tc, 29tc, 30l,
31tr, 31cl, 36l, 37tc, 37bc, 37br, 44bl, 48tl,
49tl, 52cl, 53b, 56bl, 61c, 62bl, 62br, 64br,
65tr. **Vicent Peris (OAUV/PTeam),
astrophotographer of the Astronomical
Observatory of the University of Valencia
(OAUV):** MAST, STScI, AURA, NASA - Image
processed with PixInsight at OAUV. Based on

observations made with the NASA/ESA
Hubble Space Telescope, obtained at the
Space Telescope Science Institute, which is
operated by the Association of Universities
for Research in Astronomy, Inc., under NASA
contract NAS 5-26555. 71bl. **Photolibrary:**
Corbis 64-71 (background). Science Photo
Library: 10cl, 11bl, 31bl, 34br, 38bl; Michael
Abbey 39bl; Estate of Francis Bello 60tl;
Lawrence Berkeley Laboratory 15crb; Dr Eli
Brinks 55tr; Celestial Image Co. 47c, 65bl;
Luke Dodd 46bl; Bernhard Edmaier 28cl; Dr
Fred Espenak 6-7, 8-9, 26bl; Mark Garlick
19tl, 43tr, 67br; D.Golimowski, S.Durrance
& M.Clampin 49cl; Hale Observatories 52tr;
David A Hardy 12-13, 36c, 51br; Harvard
College Observatory 19br, 43br; Jerry
Lodriguss 64bl; Claus Lunau/FOCI/Bonnier
Publications 11br; Maddox, Sutherland,
Efstathiou & Loveday 9br; Allan Morton/
Dennis Milon 54bl; MPIA-HD, Birkle, Slawik
7cr, 57tc; NASA 13tr, 28bl, 44bc; National
Optical Astonomy Observatories 21cra;
Novosti Press Agency 41br; David Parker
67cc; Ludek Pesek 34cl; Detlev Van
Ravenswaay 38cl; Royal Observatory,
Edinburgh/AAO 46-47; Rev. Ronald Royer
20-21; John Sanford 16bl, 42crb; Robin
Scagell 52br; Jerry Schad 65tl; Dan
Schechter 14cl; Dr Seth Shostak 63tl;
Eckhard Slawik 64tr; Joe Tucciarone 54-55c.
Babak A. Tafreshi: 65br.

All other images © Dorling Kindersley

For further information see:
www.dkimages.com